MW01331509

FOCUS
Your Way To
FORTUNE

Master your Mind, Enhance Your Attention,
Be Super focussed
&
Skyrocket your Productivity

Lalit Hundalani
www.lalithundalani.com
Mail: connect@lalithundalani.com

DISCLAIMER

Dedication

"To your Transformation"

"This book is dedicated to you, the reader of this book. I truly believe that you will get the value for time & money invested in procuring and reading it. I sincerely look forward to your transformation."

Table of Contents

Claim Your Free Gift!

As a token of appreciation for taking out time to read my book, I would like to offer you my E-BOOK VERSION 2.0 as a **FREE GIFT**

To claim your copy, pls visit
www.lalithundalani.com/coaching
Or
Mail to connect@lalithundalani.com

Acknowledgments

Every creative work requires the support of people around us. I am fortunate enough to have an excellent support team comprising my family, fellow authors, coaches, amazing mentors & God.

I would like to sincerely express my gratitude to the Almighty God for showering his blessings and being so kind.

My heartfelt thanks to my mother, my father, wife Nishi, son Krish, brother Rajesh, sister Veenu & nephews Mohit & Sagar, who extended their unconditional support through this journey. They took care of the other routine and essential tasks so that I could focus my attention on writing and finishing this book. Had it not been for their unwavering support, the book wouldn't have seen the light of the day.

I want to extend heartfelt gratitude to some of the fantastic individuals, as under:

My mentor & India's leading digital coach **Siddharth Rajsekhar** who took time out of his busy schedule and wrote the foreword. Truly humbled.

Mentor Arfeen Khan & Coach Naina Mansukhani for introducing me to the world of transformational life coaching & showing the way to impact lives.
Mentor Som Bathla for showing the authorpreneur path & inspiring me to become one.

Mr. **S.Kalyanaraman Iyer** & **Mr. S.Murali** for being generous enough to read the book and share the endorsements.

My nephew Mohit Ramchandani for designing the beautiful website www.lalithundalani.com.

A big thanks to all the wonderful people who contributed to this endeavor in one way or the other.

Stay Happy Stay Safe.

Lalit Hundalani

Foreword

Focus is your most valuable asset, not time. And I'm glad that **the author Lalit Hundalani** has gone deep into this subject. I had a chance to review the contents of this book, and I'm delighted to see that there is a structured system to achieve better focus and productivity.

I congratulate Lalit Hundalani for taking this initiative and coming out with this wonderful book - **"Focus Your Way To Fortune."**

When I was struggling in my business, it was **"Focus"** that got me out of that situation to build a multi-million dollar business.

The world is filled with so many "pop-ups" that many people do not know that they are distracted. Mindless scrolling of newsfeeds, checking WhatsApp messages every few seconds, and binging on YouTube and Netflix is the new normal in today's world. This is subtly affecting so many people. It defocuses people from the more essential things in life and leads to inconsistent results.

When you create more than you consume, you will get rich. And 90% of our society are consumers. It's that small 10% percentage of who achieve success because they can tap into the power of focus.

I'm glad that this book will help a lot of people with the precise formula and systems to get better in their lives.

I'm happy to be writing this foreword, and I wish **Lalit** all the best in helping people **focus their way to their fortunes**.

Wishing this book a great success!

-Siddharth Rajsekar
India's Leading Digital Coach
Amazon #1 Best Selling Author of the book "You Can Coach"

Endorsement

I have grown listening to my father using this phrase, "Practice what you Preach," and as time progressed, you start heading towards the path of "Walk the Talk." Well done, **Lalit**, for getting this book on **"Focus – your way to Fortune."** It has been riveting to read the book right from the first story of the journey of five sages to the world beckoning them. To me, you are the sage that has traveled a fascinating journey as a banking Professional 20 years back to now as a Coach, Author, and "Walking the Talk" on focus with the single pursuit of bringing a difference in people's life.

Every millennium had its own set of challenges for humanity to get their focus and pursue their goals in life. If you listen to the stories of people like Mahatma Gandhi, Martin Luther King Jr., Nelson Mandela or Swami Vivekananda, or the flying Sikh Milka Singh, it may look like it was a set of events that were bound to happen in their life. Step back, and if you take a deeper look at the events in their life, you will observe that while the event was unfolding in front of them, their awareness level was at its peak, and they started getting to FOCUS on one issue that was important to them in their life. This pursuit of getting focus has been the single decisive factor in any field. Whether you are a student, homemaker, or a professional in your area, living a king-size life is your right, and this book handholds you to achieve your dreams.

This book is a practical hack as the emerging connected world will see more opportunities to network and offer opportunities in abundance for distractions from your pursuits of life that you want to live. The technology is only going to add fury to the fire.

This book will calm the readers' minds, and a peaceful mind will be a fertile mind. What inspires me is that this book will give a reader not only just to understand the meaning of focus at a conceptual level but also a roadmap drawn to experience it and live it. For sure, as an entrepreneur, I will have this book on my table and practice every word that Lalit has explained. Remarkable, **Lalit,** for being generous to place this book for the world to learn and move forward. May your tribe grow and prosper.

Wishing this book all the success!

S.Kalyanaraman Iyer
Co-founder and CEO | Virtuoskill

Testimonial

Wow, the book" **Focus your way to Fortune**" by **Lalit Hundalani** is a ready reckoner for all fortune seekers. Fortune favors the brave is an old adage. Fortune is in one's hands and the individual self. Awakening the self within is the trigger to ensure that fortune is in the kitty. And the only mantra for this is FOCUS which is the central theme in this book.

Focus induces willpower and rejuvenates the new you. The book delineates the clarity in prioritizing the schedule, removing the clutters in mind, and having a single-point agenda. Shakespeare has rightly said, "Ambition should be made of sterner stuff," and sure one can only achieve this by greater FOCUS and make a fortune.

The book aims to drive home the means to control focus and stresses the critical role of neuroscience in preventing straying away from thoughts and bringing it back to track. The nitty-gritty issues of the various sources of distraction and how to avoid this frenzy to stay focussed are the eye-catcher The modus operandi of mastering this art by learning two critical aspects of concentration viz. awareness and mind are the best part in this book.

The importance of focusing on the blueprint of fortune is the masterstroke of Lalit in this book which carves a niche in better understanding the nuances of staying focussed.

I am glad this book will enable many youngsters with a thumb rule to make a fortune by staying focused. I am elated to scribble this testimonial and wish **Lalit Hundalani, India's leading Life Training Coach and author of the #1 bestselling book " Hacking the Productivity,"** the very best in all his endeavors.

Wishing this book all the success!

Swaminathan Murali
Specialist in Contract and Project Management
and Freelance consultant
Author of " Interpersonal Undercurrents"

"FOCUS lets you see the INVISIBLE so that you can achieve the IMPOSSIBLE."

Introduction

"Feeding distractions & starving focus leads you on the path to nowhere."

-Lalit Hundalani

The Story of Five Sages

Once upon a time, there was a village in a faraway place. The inhabitants had easy-going life with abundance all around. However, no one visited the town for two reasons:

1. *The village was located in a far-off valley among the mountains.*
2. *The way to reach the place was long and tedious.*

Many people came to know about the prosperity and the abundance of the place. They tried reaching there but gave up once they learned about the hurdles involved in the journey.

There was an old and wise sage in the village who was the source of spiritual and moral guidance. The villagers respected him greatly for all his wisdom, knowledge, and selfless service to the entire town. Sage was also very fond of the villagers, and that's why he had settled there for many years.

As he was getting older, he thought of succession planning so that people have someone to look up to, even after he has gone. Also, being a wise person, he wanted to pass the beacon of enlightenment well in time. With these thoughts in mind, he sent a message to the ashram where he originally came from.

The message was short," I am old, send one sage to whom I will transfer my learnings. Pls, ensure to send someone, mindful of distractions!"

Once the head sage received the message at the ashram, he called together all his disciples and informed them about the news. He further said that" I would like to send five of you to the village; who would like to go?" The disciples were slightly confused, and they asked why five of us when the message is for sending only one.

The head sage calmly replied, "The way to the village is long and tedious, and I am not sure that even after sending five of you, how many of you would be finally able to make it. So, I don't want to take any chances."

The young disciples were confident and argued that they were competent enough to complete
the journey and reach their destination. There was no need to send five; one was sufficient. They tried to convince the head, but he insisted and finally pushed through his idea, much to the displeasure of his disciples. Finally, five sages came forward to embark on the journey. They got the necessary instructions before starting off.

Soon after starting the journey, they reached a village where they were welcomed by the villagers wholeheartedly. The people of that village were generally good and kind-hearted. Later, they realized that the village head priest had passed away recently, and the villagers were looking for someone who could fill that position. They were willing to pay the sage who would stay back to fill in the shoes of the dead priest. It was a significant amount with perks like own house, domestic help, and support for daily necessities. One of the sages was attracted to the offer and decided to stay back. He reasoned to his colleagues that the villagers needed a spiritual guide, and being on the same path, it was his moral responsibility to help them.

The other four sages tried convincing him, but it didn't work. So, leaving him behind other four continued on their journey. The fifth one stayed back in the village with a lovely home, good food, and other riches, strictly not meant for a sage.

As the four sages moved on, they reached the outskirts of a kingdom. Incidentally, the king was passing by on his horse. The king invited the four sages to his camp for food and offered them the night stay as it was already dusk. The king was generous, and he spent time during the night listening to their stories and background.

Late into the night, the sages asked for leave so that they can go back to sleep and resume their journey the next day. As they were leaving, the king asked the youngest one to stay around for a while. When they were alone, the king told him that he was very impressed by his personality, thoughts, background, and journey. He requested him to marry his daughter, stay back in his kingdom to be his successor, and become the king when the time comes. The young sage was overwhelmed by the offer as he was not expecting any such thing. He thought that if God has given this opportunity to him, there must be some reason behind it.

In the morning, he shared last night's discussion with his three friends. He also communicated to them his decision to accept the offer. Eventually, he stayed back in the kingdom to marry the princess and became the heir apparent. After that, three sages resumed their journey.

The three sages now realized what head sage was talking about and why he insisted on sending five of them instead of one. To break the trend, they made a pact to be more vigilant. They agreed to keep a watch on each other to avoid the repetition of similar instances.

As they continued on the journey, a fierce storm broke through. They mutually decided to find a safe house to weather the storm and continue the trip once it was over. They came across a place owned by a widow lady. They requested her to allow them the shelter. She was a very kind lady, who welcomed them wholeheartedly, prepared warm meals, and arranged beds to rest.

Owing to the weather and fatigue, one of the sages fell sick. The woman requested the two friends to stay back until their friend recovered. Left with no other option and not willing to leave their friend behind, they stayed back.

The lady served three of them with all the dedication and attention. She took great care of the sick sage to ensure a fast recovery. After some days, he got better and regained his health. Three sages got together and discussed the plan to continue on their journey. The sage who had recovered recently confessed that he was very impressed by the selfless service of the landlady. He was in love with her and wanted to be with her for the rest of his life. The two tried to convince him that she was just a distraction, but the smitten sage was in no mood to listen. Realizing that convincing him was turning out to be a futile exercise, they left the house and continued further. They discussed how easily their companions were distracted from the ultimate objective. They boasted about their commitment and loyalty to the task at hand.

One day when two of them were passing by a village, suddenly a crowd surrounded them. The villagers were atheists and challenged the two sages for religious debate. One of the sages got passionate and started defending the religion. He tried desperately to win the crowd with his knowledge and wits. On the other hand, the villagers were egoistic who held great pride in their knowledge and wisdom. Not the one to take things lying down, they vehemently countered all his arguments. The debate continued for several days. Finally, with no end in sight, other sage decided that it was time to carry on. He reasoned with his friend to leave the villagers with their beliefs, as the debate was not good for them. The sage engaged in the discussion disagreed and said he would go only after proving his point to the villagers, forcing them to change their mindset and convincing them to accept his religion.

It was disheartening for his friend. He tried several times and made numerous attempts, but the other sage didn't buzz. Finally, the last sage decided to continue his journey. Within a couple of days, eventually, he reached the destination. He met the old sage and communicated his availability to start the training. The old sage asked him about his journey, and the young disciple shared the details and brought him up to date with all the happenings.

After listening carefully, the old sage smiled and said, "I see the head sage deciphered my message accurately. You see, my dear young fellow, the path to this village is not that tough, but it is full of distractions. And what we as a village have managed to achieve is not that hard to achieve. But, as you have learned on your path getting here, the secret to achieving results is to be mindful of distractions. And with that, my dear friend, we have concluded your first lesson."

Moral of the Story

It's an old story, and you might have known it earlier, but the story's moral is very much relevant in the contemporary world. We may plan to achieve great things and set elaborate goals, but things don't happen if we are not mindful of distractions. Therefore, unwavering focus on the end goal and competency to avoid distractions is a must for achieving what we want.

The story signifies the importance of focus since ancient times. These were the times when distractions were limited.

However, in modern times the elements seeking your attention are unlimited. In such a scenario, the focus has become the most crucial skill of modern times. Mastering this one skill paves the pathway to learning all other skills. It is the essential skill that can guide us through the maze of life—the master key which can unlock many doors, provide clarity and make the journey easier.

I have personally experienced the power of focus in my life. I have felt the highs when it's present and lows when it's not. Being an author and a transformation coach, a significant part of my work requires creativity, which is impossible if the focus is missing.

There was a time when it was extremely tough for me to concentrate. I struggled a lot to focus on my studies during my school days. The slightest of noise and disturbances were enough to put me off.

I would sit for hours going through the books, but the progress was plodding. I could see others devoting less time yet finishing the tasks much faster, but it required long hours for me.

Having grown in an era where the number of hours put in signified your efforts, showed your dedication, hard work, and commitment, observing others working less and achieving more was astounding. I justified that maybe these guys were talented, more intelligent, and gifted than I am. God has been partial to me, and I can't do much about it. Like most occasions, conveniently, I passed on the blame to an external force, and life carried on. In this case, it was GOD, completely unchallengeable and unapproachable.

Soon I started noticing that it was not just 1 or 2 students, but even some of my close friends and few cousins had this ability. So, I was intrigued; how is it possible?

As I grew up, I also came across the stories of successful individuals, school & college drop-outs making it big, achieving success, and creating enormous wealth.

At the global level, the success stories of personalities like Bill Gates (Microsoft), Paul Allen (Microsoft), Michael Dell (Dell Computers), Mark Zuckerberg (Facebook), Steve Jobs (Apple), Jack Dorsey (Twitter), Jan Koum (What's app) were the talk of the town.

Closer home, there were people like Azim Premji (Wipro), Dhirubhai Ambani(Reliance Group), Mukesh Jagtiani(Landmark Group), Sachin Tendulkar(Sports-Cricket), Aamir Khan(Movie star). They created ripples by achieving massive success in their respective fields without completing a formal college education.

This broke another notion that completing formal education is very important to become successful in life. It was not. It became more puzzling for me.

Earlier it was one question, now there were many:

- Why is it that sometimes it becomes easier for us to do a task while at other times, the same activity stretches indefinitely?
- How is it that some people work less but still accomplish more in less time?
- How is it that someone who has not completed formal education becomes super successful while the one with good grades and degrees continues to slog?
- What differentiates a successful person from an ordinary one?
- What is the most critical thing which helps in the creation of a fortune?

The quest to find the answers continued till I found that all these questions had a common thread, which was indeed the answer to all these questions.

The answer was **FOCUS**.

- ✓ When we are focused and concentrated on our job, we can accomplish it much faster.
- ✓ People with high focus skills accomplish more in less time.
- ✓ Single-minded, unwavering focus on their goals allowed school & college drop-outs to achieve massive success.
- ✓ The vagaries of life can distract an ordinary person but not the focussed one. Like the story of 5 sages, one who can cut through distractions is the one who reaches his destination.

Focus is what leads to the creation of a **Fortune.**

The Focus to Fortune pyramid on the next page connects the dots and offers a pictorial representation of the path to be followed.

Let's check it out.

Focus To Fortune Pyramid

In case you had not known this earlier, I am sure now you would have realized the significance of focus as a skill. So much needed but largely ignored.

Why should you read this book?

The book broadly covers all the critical aspects of focus, its importance, and its role in paving the path to success. Having read this book, you will get clarity on the below points:

- ✓ What is Focus?
- ✓ How can it help in the creation of fortune?
- ✓ What is the relevance of focus in the modern world?
- ✓ What is the importance of focus in day-to-day life?
- ✓ Why do we need to focus in our life?
- ✓ Why is it difficult to focus?
- ✓ What are the various factors impacting focus?
- ✓ How can we master the focus?
- ✓ How to train our minds for focus?
- ✓ How to train our body?
- ✓ How to manage the external environment?
- ✓ 10 step Focus to Fortune blueprint
- ✓ Bonus hacks to sharpen the focus

I have made a sincere attempt to go into as much depth as possible. Each chapter has a summary that serves as the ready reckoner and assignments to get you into action.

The objective of presenting this book is to help you transform into a more focused person and become a better version of yourself.

Any transformation has two pre-requisites:

I. **Awareness & Knowledge**: This is my deliverable, and I will ensure that you get the required information, tools, techniques, and a step-by-step blueprint for giving you exact clarity as to what needs to be done.

II. **Action**: This is your deliverable. Once you get clarity on:

- ✓ What needs to be done
- ✓ Why it needs to be done and
- ✓ How it needs to be done.

The next logical step is to leap into action.

It is the action where most people fail. There is no dearth of knowledge and information, but it is the most important reason people don't get results or change doesn't happen. What good is knowledge if you are not applying it? Knowledge without application is similar to money in the money box; it can't multiply independently. You get returns only when you act and invest it.

So, get out of the box to grow.

I have provided assignments at the end of each chapter to make things easier for you and ensure that you don't lose focus. My sincere request is to do these assignments religiously. The way, you need to follow the right recipe to cook your favorite dish; the same case here. The formula to maximize value and extract the most from this book would require you to:

1. Understand Concepts
2. Acquire Knowledge
3. Do Assignments
4. Take action
5. Apply knowledge
6. Measure Results

7. Review, Rework & Repeat

It always helps to have the company of the right kind of people on a similar journey like you. This inspires you, motivates you, and keeps you on track when you feel low and feel like giving up.

Fortunately for you, I have a community of action takers committed to act and transform.

To fast-track your journey, you can join the **VIP Facebook group**-VERSION 2.0 CLUB.

Join the Facebook group here >>VERSION 2.0 CLUB.

Or type

https://www.facebook.com/groups/465486904543970/ in your web browser to join it.

You are indeed an action taker. Compliments to you for joining in; let's begin the journey now.

Introduction: Synopsis

- **Focus** is a crucial element that helps us to concentrate on our task and accomplish it faster.

- **Clarity** of goals and single-minded focus enables people to be super successful despite not completing a formal education.

- **Focus** differentiates an ordinary person from the extraordinary one.

- **To reach** the final destination, you must cut through the distractions.

- **Mastering** the focus allows you to make a **Fortune**.

- **Four steps** to master the focus are knowing:

    - What is focus?

    - Why do we need to focus?

    - Why can't we focus?

    - How to focus?

- There are **two critical elements** of any transformation:

    1.Awareness: Knowing what you don't know.

    2.Action: Application of the knowledge.

Assignment 1

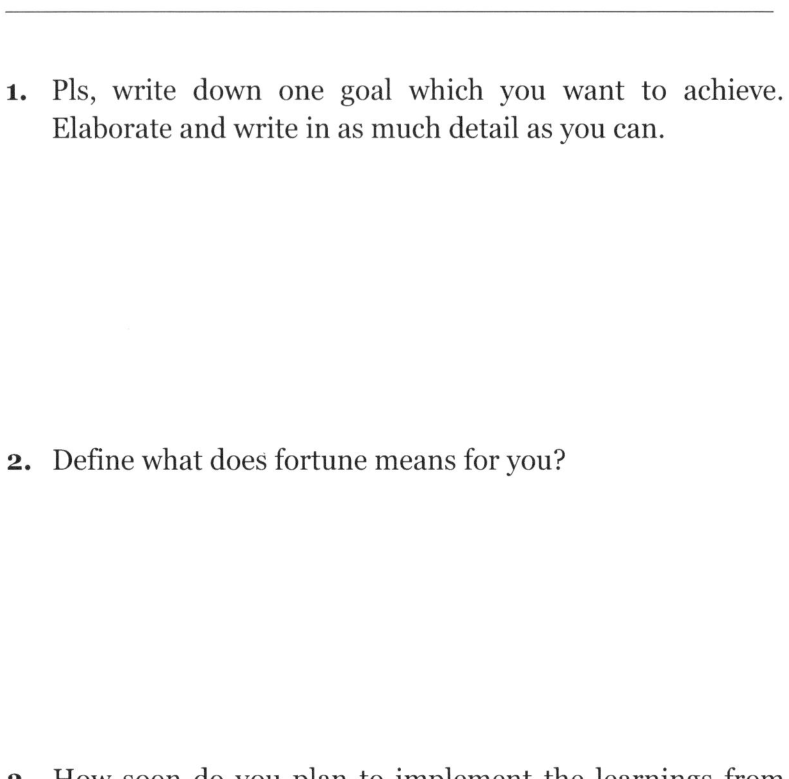

1. Pls, write down one goal which you want to achieve. Elaborate and write in as much detail as you can.

2. Define what does fortune means for you?

3. How soon do you plan to implement the learnings from this book?

Chapter 1:What is Focus ?

"FOCUS is Following One Course Until Success"

-Lalit Hundalani

Defining Focus

The Merriam Webster dictionary enumerates the various definitions of focus as under:

- ✓ A center of activity, attraction, or attention.
- ✓ A point of concentration.
- ✓ Directed attention.
- ✓ A state or condition permitting clear perception or understanding.
- ✓ Adjustment for distinct visions.
- ✓ A point at which rays (of light, heat, or sound) converge or from which they diverge or appear to diverge.
- ✓ A point of convergence of a beam of particles (such as electrons)
- ✓ To cause or to be concentrated.

The first known usage of the word focus dates back to the year 1664. As per experts' focus is the act of concentrating your interest or activity on something. In simple terms, the focus is directed attention. When we focus on something, we concentrate our attention or effort on that thing. By the very definition, it's evident that we must ignore several other things to focus our attention and energy on one thing. It is also defined as the thinking skill that enables people to overcome procrastination, act, continue the attention and effort till the completion of a task.

In a village, there lived a wise man. He was known for his wisdom and always used to share knowledge with fellow villagers. He used to meditate daily and always inspired others to do so. Villagers respected him a lot for his wisdom and ability to meditate for hours at length. Once, he was meditating in the forest when he heard the faint sound of a woman's anklet. Gradually the sound became more apparent, and he could make out that woman was walking towards him. Finally, after some time, she reached very close and brushed past him. At this moment, the man opened his eyes. He was annoyed as the lady broke his concentration.

He called the woman and questioned her," Couldn't you see; I was meditating here? Why did you hit me?"

To this woman innocently replied," Did I? I don't even remember seeing you?

The man said," Yes, it was just a while ago. "

The woman replied, "I am sorry for the mistake, I think I didn't notice you, and that's why the incident happened." She further added," I am going to meet my lover who is waiting for me, and that's why I am overjoyed."

The man was surprised and asked her," I was meditating, but I could hear the sound of your anklet and feel your presence. You were walking with your eyes wide open; how could you miss me?"

The woman replied," As I mentioned earlier, I was elated and excited to meet my lover. However, I could see no one but him and wanted to meet him at the earliest. I was not aware of the environment or the surroundings; that's why I seemed to have missed you."

She further continued, "I am sorry, but since you mentioned that you were meditating and concentrating, if that be the case, then you should have been oblivious of my presence and shouldn't have been disturbed."

This was a moment of a rude awakening for the wise man. He realized that the woman with her eyes open was much more focused on her goal than him. He was distracted by her presence while she wasn't. So, he decided to practice more before preaching to others till he mastered this art.

The moral of the story:

- Choose what to focus upon.
- The object of your attention should be exciting enough to mesmerize and hold your focus for long.
- Once you are focused on something then, you can't be distracted by your environment.

While it may sound simple to concentrate attention on one thing, it isn't. Sometimes simplest of things are the toughest to follow; the same is the case with focus. Most of us struggle to concentrate on a single thing for long since the mind starts to wander in different directions. Hence the importance of focus can't be estimated enough.
The ability to focus attention is one of the most important abilities one should possess. However, most people cannot concentrate. Their attention usually wanders, not being able to stay on one subject for any reasonable period.

As stated earlier, I was among those people who struggled big time while trying to focus. I still remember my situation while trying to focus on my studies in my growing up years. From the chirping of a bird to the sound of thunder, children playing outside, to the sound of a song being played on a loudspeaker, anything and everything was just enough to distract me. So often, I used to ask myself:

- How can I focus better on my studies?
- How can I learn faster?
- How can I avoid making errors?
- How can I be more efficient?
- How can I improve my memory?

Well, all I could know then was that I should concentrate better, but how was missing.

Over the years, I have realized that the ability to focus can be developed like any other skill. A person who trains his or her mind can concentrate without being distracted by thoughts, noises, or anything else. One of the main objectives of writing this book is to address the how part of FOCUS, which troubled me for a more significant part of my life. Here I intend to share the techniques, which work in improving focus and concentration. Sounds good? I am sure it does.

Focus is an essential thinking skill that allows one to get on with a task and maintain attention and effort until completion. So, if you're wondering how to focus better, it's a skill that has to be consistently worked upon. Think about focus in terms of running. You can't just wake up one day and decide to run a marathon; you have to work towards and train for it.

"Focus is the leash which is essential to tame the mind, lest it goes berserk."

Focus in the Contemporary Scenario

One day the legendary Warren Buffett asked his pilot Mike flint to perform a simple exercise.

He asked him to write down his top 25 career goals. Flint took some time to jot them down.

After that, Buffett asked Flint to go over his list and circle his top five objectives. Flint retook his time, going over the list and eventually deciding on his top five priorities.

Flint had two lists at this period. List A consisted of the five items he had circled, while List B consisted of the 20 items he had not circled.

Flint stated that he would immediately begin working on his top five priorities in list A. Buffett then inquired about the second list, asking, "And what about the ones you didn't circle?"

"Well, the top 5 are my major emphasis, but the other 20 are a close second," Flint answered. Nevertheless, they're still vital, so I'll continue to work on them as needed. Although they are not as essential, I intend to devote my full attention to them."

"No, Mike," Buffett said. He added," Everything you didn't circle became your list of things to avoid at all costs. No matter what, you're not going to pay attention to these things until you've completed your top five."

This method is famously known as the **warren buffet's 5/25 elimination rule**. It is an effective way of arriving at priorities by way of eliminations. You learn what to do and also what not to do. Everything except the top 5 in the list is what shouldn't be done.

The current age is an information age, where we are continuously bombarded with information. There were times when we used to seek news; now, it's the other way around. Unless you are living under a rock, the chances are that you will have the updates of all that matters and, in some instances, all that doesn't matter as well. With so much happening around and the continuous stream of information flowing endlessly, it won't be wrong to term the current age as the **"Age of Distraction."**

Most people's typical means of distraction are mobile phones, social media applications, television OTT platforms, email notifications, and virtual meetings or conference calls. Everyone and everything is competing for attention, and therefore it's challenging to limit the disruptions and carry on with the meaningful work.

Dr. Sophie Leroy, associate Professor of the Management University of Washington Bothell, has coined the term attention residue to help explain situations where people find it challenging to be focused on the task at hand. According to his research, the brain generally finds it difficult to switch between tasks. As we change from Task A to Task B, part of the attention often stays with Task A instead of fully transferring to Task B; this is what he terms as **attention residue**.
Here attention is split between the ongoing task at hand and the earlier task.

Attention residue quickly occurs when we leave tasks unfinished when we get interrupted or anticipate that we will have to rush to get it done once we have a chance to get to the incomplete or pending work. Our brain finds it hard to let go of these tasks and keeps them active in the back of our minds, even when we are trying to focus on and perform other tasks.

Going back to the analogy of Task A and Task B, when we experience attention residue and keep thinking about Task A while working on Task B, it means we have fewer cognitive resources available to perform Task B. The impact? Our performance on Task B is likely to suffer, especially if Task B is cognitively demanding.

Essentially what it implies is that distractions or multitasking restricts the ability to focus. Rather than working on multiple tasks simultaneously, neither of which is complete. A better option would be to finish the job at hand and then move on to the next position. No unfinished task, no attention residue. A potent yet straightforward outcome.

This also proves the theory of **Doing One Thing At A Time (DOTAT),** once again.

We have got ample clarity on the focus and its relevance in the contemporary world. In the next chapter, we will cover:

- ✓ Why it is essential to focus.
- ✓ We will get into details of microfocus & macro focus.
- ✓ Visit life-transforming anecdotes from the lives of compelling & successful personalities.
- ✓ We will also cover scenarios where focus and concentration are a must & non-negotiable at any cost.

Let's flip over and move on.

Chapter 1:Synopsis

- **Focus** is directed attention. It is the act of concentrating attention or effort on one single thing. We must ignore several other things to focus our attention and energy on one thing. It is the thinking skill that helps overcome procrastination, act, and continue the attention and effort until completing a task.

- **Doing One Thing At A Time (DOTAT)** is an essential principle of focus.

- **Warren Buffet's 5/25** rule of elimination is an excellent way to identify the priorities and decide what to focus on.

    - Make a list of 25 goals
    - Circle the top 5 goals
    - Write the top 5 goals in list A.
    - Write the remaining 20 in the list B.
    - Focus on achieving the goals in list A.
    - Move to list B, only once list A is complete

- The current era is known as the **Age of Distraction**. This is because there are so many things vying for our attention. Without mastering the art of focus, it's challenging to achieve anything meaningful without losing the plot.

- **Attention Residue** occurs during multi-tasking when we shift from one task to another without completing the first task. As a result, the second task only gets partial attention since some attention is still engaged in task one. This doesn't allow the focus and causes distraction.

Assignment 2

---

1. Use Warren buffet's 5/25 rule to identify your top 5 priorities.

2. Write the instances where you routinely do multitasking.

3. How will you quit multitasking?

Chapter 2

Why do we need to Focus?

"You become what you focus on, so focus on what you want to become."

-Lalit Hundalani

FOCUS is one key element, the absence or presence of which has far-reaching effects in all the areas of our life. It can make us, and it can break us.

One reason why focus is required or why there is so much renewed interest and emphasis is its connection with our mind. It is said that things happen twice, first in our minds and then in reality. So, whatever we want to achieve needs to be focussed upon.

Focus on scarcity, problems, pain, suffering, misery, and you get loads of it.

Focus on abundance, solutions, pleasure, wealth, growth, happiness, and attract them.

For this reason, it's said that you must focus on what you want and not on what you don't want. Unfortunately, natural human behavior instigates us to keep talking about the not-so-good things, criticize and engage in negative self-talk. This shapes our thoughts, and we continue to focus on all that negativity and continue to fail. To let the mind focus on positivity, conscious effort and training are required. It doesn't happen on its own.

Whether it's academics, reading, sports, work, drive, workout, yoga, meditation, cooking, or any other activity, the focus is a pre-requisite.

Broadly the critical importance of focus can be owed to two key factors:

- ✓ Achieving Excellence
- ✓ Averting Disaster

Let's have a look at both the factors in detail to understand them better.

Achieving Excellence

Since ancient times, human civilization has realized the importance of this skill, and all the great warriors were made to practice and master this technique.

Our religious books and epics are full of numerous such examples. One such illustration is beautifully described in the epic Mahabharata.
When Dronacharya was teaching archery to his students, he once asked them to shoot a bird on the tree by aiming its eye.

He called all of them one by one, and showing the bird, he asked them what they saw.

Everyone except Arjuna said they saw the tree, the branches, the bird, etc., so everyone missed the target.

Arjuna had been practicing archery day and night and was the best archer among the students of Dronacharya.

So, when Arjuna's turn came, Drona inquired him as follows:

Drona: "What do you see?"

Arjuna: "I see the eye of the bird."

Drona: "Do you see the tree?"

Arjuna: "No"

Drona: "Do you see the branch?"

Arjuna: "No"

Drona: "Do you see the bird?"

Arjuna: "No"

Drona: "Then what else do you see, Arjuna?"
Arjuna: "Nothing.
Saying so, Arjuna released the arrow, and it just hit the target straight.

The moral of the story is straightforward. Intense focus on your target allows you to ignore the distracting environment and achieve the desired outcome.

Focus lets us excel both at the macro as well as micro-level.

Macro & Micro application of focus

At a macro level, focus on the end goal or purpose of life ensures that we consistently move in a single direction, unperturbed by the numerous distractions vying for our attention. The stories of all the successful individuals worldwide have time and again proved that a unidirectional focus lets you continue on your chosen path till you reach your destination. Life will continue to test in its own way. There would be times when you will come across opportunities trying to lure you and change course. There would be obstacles trying to stop you and give up on the pursuit of your goals. Focus ensures you don't give up in such circumstances.

Let's understand the macro application of focus with the help of few illustrations:

Illustration 1: Former Indian cricket captain- Sourav Ganguly

Famous cricketer and former Indian Captain Sourav Ganguly used to play football in his early days, and he was good at it. But once he started playing cricket, he continued with this sport only. The journey was not easy for him. After his debut, he couldn't perform in international cricket on expected lines. He was out of the Indian team for several years. If he didn't have a strong focus, he would have given up and gone ahead to pursue an alternate career. He was very young at the time of his debut and had his whole life in front of him. However, he didn't lose focus; he continued to practice and sharpen his skills. He performed exceptionally well in domestic leagues, which paved his return to the national cricket team. Later, he became the captain and led the unit successfully. He went on to become one of the most successful captains in Indian cricket history.

Illustration 2: Former Mr. Universe & Hollywood actor-Arnold Schwarzenegger

When Arnold decided to pursue bodybuilding, he was discouraged by many people. However, he was undeterred, committed to his goal, and focused on his approach. That's what helped him transform from an ordinary lanky lad to a macho man, who went on to become Mr. Universe and won the title not only once or twice but seven times.

He proved his mettle again when he decided to foray into Hollywood and become an actor. Of course, there were naysayers, people who wanted to discourage him, mocked him for his physique and built, criticized him for his acting skills and other stuff. But, not the one to give up easily, he kept his focus on what he wanted to achieve and went on to accomplish unprecedented success.

Illustration 3: Former Indian captain and Cricketer Sachin Tendulkar

Sachin Tendulkar is immensely talented; he was indeed a child prodigy who knew he wanted to play cricket since early childhood. He was one of the youngest players to debut in international cricket and became a cricketing legend. He had one of the most illustrious cricket careers, but even he hit the rough patch. In the late 90's he became the captain of the Indian cricket team. However, under his leadership, the team performance was not up to the mark. There were more losses than wins. This started affecting his performance as a player.

Soon he realized that captaincy had shifted the focus from his game to team administration, and he could not justify either. So, he voluntarily gave up the captaincy, focused on his game, and shined again. During those days, experts had written him off and were eager to bid him farewell. Through his sheer focus, he continued playing cricket, achieved numerous milestones, and remained an integral part of the national cricket team for more than a decade. He had one of the longest playing stints, which lasted for more than 2.5 decades.

Numerous such success stories prove that focus precedes excellence, irrespective of what you do and where you are. It's the single most critical trait which is shared among all the extraordinary individuals.

In the illustrations shared above, nothing happened overnight. It was the focus on small things, work on the small nuances, minute details that created magic for them. Whether it was Sourav Ganguly or Arnold Schwarzenegger, or Sachin Tendulkar, they focused on daily routines and sharpened their skills. Focus on each day, concentration on each task at hand eventually contributed to the final outcome. They all had focus which led them to create a fortune for themselves.

While trying to focus, the biggest problem we face is controlling the mind from wandering out. For excelling in any job, focus and one-pointed unwavering attention of the mind on the job is a must.

To realize the outcome, it's equally essential to focus on the task at hand with total concentration until it is completed successfully. Every single accomplishment takes us closer to the fulfillment of our purpose. Consider your purpose to be the summit of a mountain. To scale the peak, focusing on the path which leads towards it is a must. It requires a combination of keeping the bigger goal in mind, focusing on daily actions/tasks, and doing the stuff that takes you closer to it.

For example, my goal is to complete the book and publish it by x date. To ensure that I achieve my outcome, I have decided that I will write 1000 words/per day. Thus, I am focused on my end goal, say, next month (fingers crossed), which pushes me to focus on my daily task (I am close to it, by the way).

As I am writing these lines, it's around midnight, I am feeling tired, it's slightly challenging to concentrate, and I want to go to bed. These are the distractions, but since I have finalized the publishing date for this book and am very much focused on it, I can force myself and keep writing.

In a nutshell, mastering the Micro-Focus (daily tasks) makes us excel in Macro Focus (Ultimate Outcome).

If I have to summarize it, I would like to refer to the Focus to Fortune pyramid shared in the introduction.

Averting Failures

In the previous section, we evaluated the positives of having a focus. We enumerated how the presence of focus can help us in becoming successful and live an extraordinary life. Now, we will spend some time and see what the absence of direction can do.

Once, there was a king who believed that his kingdom would grow and prosper if his countrymen would better themselves by gaining experience and enhancing knowledge in their interest areas. He believed that anyone who follows passion and does a business out of it could contribute more to the kingdom as compared to the cost kingdom would incur to help that person get to that point. So, the king provided education, security, jobs, money, and other resources to focus on their passion and not worry about earning or making a living right away.

Most of the king's countrymen took advantage of what the king was offering them. But there were exceptions. Some people only saw obstacles and made excuses about how they have other priorities. One such person was the king's childhood friend. He never did anything more than he had to get by. One Sunday, while the king and his friend were having breakfast at the king's palace, the king's friend again complained about how hard it was to earn enough money and how hard it was to get a better job.

The king then asked the friend, "Why don't you learn new skills so you would be able to apply for better jobs?"

The friend just shook his head and mumbled, "I don't have time for that."

The king looked at his friend with a smile and replied, "Well, my friend, I believe you have a big problem with focus and setting priorities."

The friend got upset and replied, "It's easy for you to say and judge me. You are the king, and you were born rich. You never had to work, study, or do any work to provide for your family."

The king still had a smile on his face even though his friend was rude. He looked his friend in the eye and made an offer to prove his point, "Ok, if that is what you think, let's try something. You may go into my treasury right now and collect as much wealth as you can. But you only have time to do so until sunset."

The king's friend couldn't believe his luck. He was overwhelmed at the opportunity. As soon as he calmed down, he sat next to the king and suggested a toast, "To my dear friend, who helped me change my life. We must drink to that! We need wine, lots of wine; we must celebrate!"

The king tried to calm down his friend and remind him of his deadline. But the friend explained to the king, "Don't worry. I have more than enough time. But, first, we must celebrate!" The king looked at his friend and pointed out what he said not that long ago, "I believe you have a problem with focus and setting priorities and not with finding opportunities. But do as you wish."

The friend just ignored the king's words and continued drinking and toasting with everyone in the palace to his good fortune.

After the king's friend spent a couple of hours drinking, eating, and toasting with everyone, he decided it was time to go home and tell his wife how their lives are about to change. Once he got home, he told his wife what happened. Both of them were so happy that they needed to celebrate their good fortune. So, they toasted, drank, and eaten until they fell asleep. After a couple of hours in the late afternoon, the king's friend finally decided to pick up some bags and go to the palace to get his fortune. On the way there, he felt so tired because of all the drinking and eating he needed to rest quickly. After an hour or so of sleeping, he got up and was back on his way to the palace. Right before the court, he saw a man doing magic tricks. Of course, this was very interesting; he asked the magician to perform some of his favorite tricks and promised him to pay once he was back. And so, another hour or so went by before the sun was starting to set.

Suddenly the king's friend realized how late he was and he started running towards the palace. On reaching there, he found that gates were shut. He demanded to see the king and wouldn't calm down until the king came to see him. Once the king went to the palace entrance, his friend pleaded with him to let him enter the treasury and take what was rightfully his. But the king wouldn't let him pass and calmly reminded his friend of the time constraint of his task.

The friend raged and yelled at the king, "This is not fair; you promised me a fortune, now you are taking back your word. The day is not over; it is not midnight. You are a liar; you don't want me to be rich or successful, you are against me, you are not my friend."

The king calmly replied, "Dear friend, I have given you an opportunity of a lifetime, and instead of focusing on it, you rather threw away your precious time for things that were not important at that time. I also warned you about setting priorities, but you ignored me."

The friend was shocked at the answer and replied, "But you were drinking and eating with me. You tricked me into wasting my time."

"No, my dear friend," elaborated the king, "If you remember, I have warned you to mind your time and focus on the opportunity in front of you. And since you didn't want to listen to me, there was nothing I could have done but to leave you to your choices and hope that you, at the end of the day, at least learn a life-changing lesson, if not leverage a life-changing opportunity. This is my gift to you. I hope you are more mindful about setting priorities in the future. Opportunities will come, my friend; you only need to be able to see them and take advantage of them in time." And so, the king's friend went home with a different kind of treasure than he expected.

The message from the story is compelling. We may get all the opportunities in the world, but they won't mean a thing unless we are focused enough to take action towards them.

Lack of focus doesn't allow you to take advantage of the best opportunities, which might come your way. Without direction, you miss out on accomplishing what you want to achieve.

Let's go through a kid's story, which drives home the point like no other.

Once there were three friends, a tortoise, and two cranes. Three of them lived near a lake, surrounded by the greenery, and fulfilled all their requirements of food & shelter. The three bonded well and were having a good time. One day while they were chatting, one of the cranes reminded everyone that soon summer would be there and the lake would go dry. It will be difficult for them to survive, so they need to figure out something. After some thinking and discussion, they concluded that cranes would fly and check for an appropriate place nearby to spend their summers. If they liked the site, they would stay; otherwise, they would come back once it was over. The next day, the two cranes flew away and, after intense searching and checking out several places, finally found a place, which was ideal for their requirements. The two came back in the evening and shared the details with their friend tortoise.

The tortoise was delighted to know about the new abode and proposed that three of them should plan to migrate at the earliest, without waiting for the onset of the summer season. To which one of the cranes pointed out that there was one problem with this plan. On being asked by the other two, he shared his concern that the place was far-off, and while cranes could fly and reach the destination conveniently, the tortoise could not do so. The other two agreed and started to think hard. After some contemplation, the tortoise came with an idea and shared it with them. The plan was to find a twig or branch of the tree, which the cranes can hold in their mouth from both ends and fly. The tortoise will have it in his mouth from the middle. This way, three of them can fly away together and reach the destination conveniently.

Cranes listened to the idea and liked it but issued a caveat. For the plan to work, it was imperative that they remained quiet during the journey and didn't open the mouth. If anyone opened their mouth for any reason, the tortoise will fall and lose its life. To which tortoise replied that he was wise enough to understand and would ensure that his mouth remained shut, all through.

They finalized the plan, and the following day, cranes started searching for the twig of the tree, which they were able to find pretty soon. Finally, they decided to commence the journey in the mid-morning to reach their new home before sunset.

As they were flying, they crossed several villages. They could hear the chatter of people below, children playing merrily, and other distractions. They chose to continue without reacting and concentrated on their journey. The tortoise was thinking that his friends were unnecessarily worried before starting the journey and underestimated his focus. With these thoughts in mind, he decided to share his feelings with them and opened his mouth.

As soon he did that, he lost the grip of the twig, which he was holding in his mouth. Before cranes could understand what happened and react, he fell and lost his life.

The cranes were heartbroken at the fate of their dear friend but couldn't do anything. They had already warned him, but he couldn't sustain his focus till the end. While he could shield himself from the external disturbances, self-pride and self-talk broke his concentration.

The story illustrates the dire consequences of losing focus in critical events, where it's a matter of life and death. While this was a fictional story, there is no shortage of real-life situations where we come across similar circumstances. Unfortunately, consequences are identical, whether it's a fictional story or real life.

To understand it better, let's consider certain real-life situations where you just can't afford to miss the focus:

Can you imagine the repercussions, what will happen?

- If a surgeon operating on a critical patient in an ICU is tired and loses focus.

- The driver of a racing car gets distracted by a phone call.

- A rope walker gets disturbed by noise while performing.

- A fighter pilot on the mission fails to fire when he must.

- A trapeze artist loses concentration for a split second during the act.

- A tourist bus driver on an uphill journey takes a wrong detour and gets off the road.

These are no-brainers. The absence of focus in any of the above situations will result in loss, pain, misery, calamity, loss of lives, etc. Missing the focus is not an option in any of these circumstances owing to the dangers involved. Distraction or loss of concentration could be for a fraction of a second, but the results can be fatal, leading to significant property loss and human lives. The mere thought of such a situation is enough to make one wet below the ears.Earlier, we saw Focus to Fortune pyramid; now, let's look at the other side of it or the wheel of No Focus, No Fortune.

No Focus-No Fortune Wheel

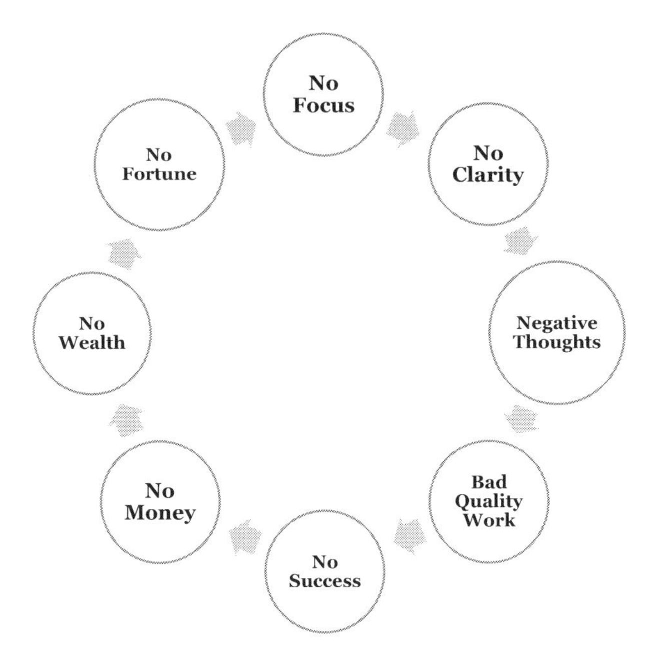

I suggest you click a pic or take a screenshot of the **Focus to Fortune pyramid** and **No Focus, No Fortune wheel**. Keep them handy with you on your mobile. Then, whenever distractions attract you, or you tend to lose focus, look at these pics. The vision of consequences will herd you back on track.

Importance of Focus

Focus has its importance in almost every area of life. It is one skill that is omnipotent and omnipresent. It can help you when you need to focus on your studies when you read, work, drive, get tasks done, meditate, and everything else.

It is the gateway to all thinking abilities, which includes but is not limited to perception, memory, learning, reasoning, problem-solving, and decision making. The absence of focus adversely impacts all aspects of our ability. Lack of concentration at work increases distraction by limiting the ability to concentrate on the right things. The effectiveness suffers badly, and the capability of getting the job done takes a hit. Mind-wandering leads to wastage of time, which translates into work not being completed or the time taken for completion is significantly higher. Either way, it's counterproductive for efficiency as the quality and quantity suffer badly.

If I have to list down the top 10 benefits of having a good focus, it would include:

1. Controlling the Mind
2. Improving the memory & concentration
3. Creative Imagination
4. More clarity
5. Enhanced Self-Awareness
6. Feeling of positivity
7. Better Decision Making
8. Better Problem-Solving Skills
9. Minimizing errors
10. High Efficiency

It always helps to focus Inside-Out, which means that we must focus internally to attain clarity, be self-aware, and develop control over our minds and actions. Once we have mastered the internal focus, we can focus on our goals and activities. As we will discuss in the latter part of the book, the trinity of mind, body, and environment plays a fundamental role in deciding the intensity of our focus. Whether we are good at it or not so good at it is primarily determined by control over mind and body, part of our internal self. A better command over our inner being allows us to manage the external environment better. We can control and command ourselves, but outside, it's the influence that works and yields results—effective control over self-ensures better management outside.

The only person you can change is no one but yourself. It is your focus which determines whether you can do it conveniently or not. Being a life transformation coach, I started transforming myself to attain the results in areas I lacked. If I couldn't do it for myself, helping others achieve transformation won't be possible.

I am a firm believer in the fact that the journey starts with you.

You got to be laser-focused on getting anything done.

Successful people are not great at everything; they are just great at one thing.

Let's hear it out from the successful people and look at the real-world examples to evaluate what a laser focus means and what it can do for you.

- ✓ James Cameroon, who made the movie AVATAR, was focused on the project for four years. Most of us are aware, how successful the project was and the cult it created. However, the capacity to remain focused on a single project for four years is not easy. It requires a lot of hard work, which eventually paid off for him in abundance.

- ✓ Larry Page, the founder of Google, states, "You should focus on one important goal, and you need to be pretty single-minded about it."

- ✓ Tom Monaghan's founder of Domino's Pizza, advocates a passionate focus on doing one thing well.

✓ According to Bill Gates, co-founder of Microsoft," If you want to be a great software company, you have to be only a software company."

✓ Jennifer Mather, animal behaviorist, biologist, and psychologist, says, "I have a ferocious ability to concentrate. I can say," I am going to do this and shut the rest of the world ."

✓ Jeong Kim, president of Lucent Technologies, once said," I can work day and night and maintain concentration without getting burned out."

✓ Stephen King, the bestselling author, says if you want to be a writer or an author, there should be no TV, Mobile, or other distractions around you. Eliminate all possible distractions.

✓ Ace investor Warren Buffet became one of the richest men by living in a constant state of no distractions.

The list can go on and on, reaffirming the single most crucial thing: focus helps succeed, whether it's long-term focus or short-term concentration.

The Focus-Success equation can therefore be summarized as:

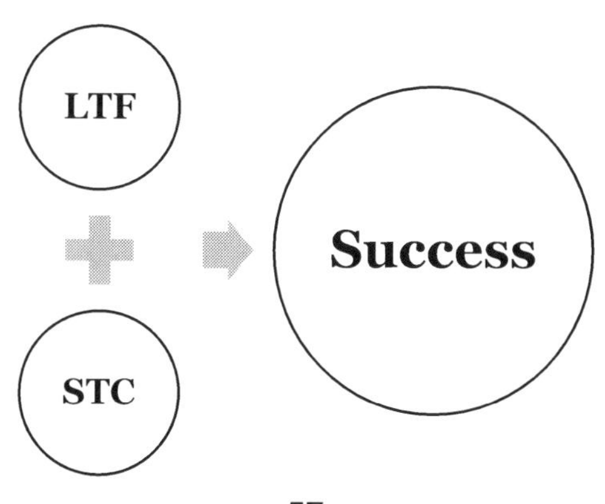

Focus-Success Equation

(LTF= Long Term Focus; STC=Short Term Concentration)

With this, we come to the end of this chapter, which was all about discovering the "Why" of focus.

As we cruise to the next chapter, get ready for intense learning and deep insights. In the next section, we will identify the limiting factors or obstructions to focus.

Trust you have been doing the assignments all along. If not, then pls go back and complete before you continue. And yes, you need to complete the worksheet for this chapter as well. Join me in the next section once done.

Chapter 2:Synopsis

- **Focus** a crucial element, the absence or presence of which has far-reaching effects in all the areas of our life. It can make us, and it can break us.

- **Mind** and **focus** have a strong connection. Therefore, focus on positive thoughts gets the favorable outcome and vice-versa.

- The critical importance of focus can be broadly classified into two segments:

    - **Achieving Excellence**: Individuals with high command of focus have excelled in their chosen area, which helped them create a fortune. To achieve success, focus is a must.

    - **Averting Disaster**: High focus tasks and jobs require excellent focus mastery and concentration. Loss of attention in such situations has disastrous repercussions.

- **No Focus** leads to **No Fortune**.

- **Top 10** benefits of focus.

    - ✓ Controlling the Mind
    - ✓ Improving the memory & concentration
    - ✓ Creative Imagination
    - ✓ More Clarity
    - ✓ Enhanced Self-Awareness

- ✓ Feeling of positivity
- ✓ Better Decision Making
- ✓ Better Problem-Solving Skills
- ✓ Minimizing errors
- ✓ High Efficiency

- ❖ To achieve the ultimate goal, we require **Long Term Focus (LTF).**

- ❖ To excel in daily tasks, we need to sharpen **Short Term Concentration. (STF)**

Long Term Focus (LTF)+Short Term Concentration (STF)=Success

Assignment 3

---

1. Which are the critical areas of your life where you have been missing the focus?

2. Which are the routine activities where you struggle to concentrate?

3.How will improving the focus and concentration in areas/activities mentioned above change your life?

Chapter 3

Why is it difficult to Focus?

"Anything worthwhile is not easy."

-Lalit Hundalani

In the earlier sections, we covered various aspects of focus, which included :

- What is focus,
- Why is it essential
- The positive outcomes of having it
- Not so positive consequences, if it's lacking
- Micro-Focus & Macro Focus
- Scenarios where it is absolutely essential and non-negotiable
- The role it plays in attracting success
- How it enables the creation of a FORTUNE
- Focus to Fortune pyramid
- No Focus, No Fortune wheel
- Focus-Success Equation
- And much more.

A natural question comes to mind: if it is an essential ingredient of achieving success and creating fortune, why don't we focus? I am yet to find someone who doesn't aspire for success or wealth. So if it is the master key to so many locks, why not get it?
The answer is not very difficult. Just like many other great things in life, it doesn't come easy. It might look easy, but it is far from it. Most of us want to achieve great things but shy away from working hard and follow the correct process. We want everything to happen within our comfort zone.

In this section, we will understand why it isn't easy to focus and the obstacles involved.

Factors responsible for deciding the state of our focus can be broadly classified into two categories:

- Internal state factors

- External state factors

Internal State Factors

Internal State includes the factors which comprise our inner self and can be controlled by us. It contains two critical components-our mind and our body. Mind (Psychological) & Body (Physiological) define the internal reasons for the presence of focus or its lack.

Let us understand the cause & effect relationship between these factors and focus.

1) Psychology of Focus(State of Mind): It's a very vast topic and encompasses various elements like our emotional states(Positive & negative), mind wandering, self-doubt, brain alertness, etc. We will cover all these elements in-depth to have better insights into cause & effect relationships. Once we know why can't we focus, it would be easier to address the how part of it, in the next chapter. To understand the psychology of focus in detail, we will cover the following areas:

a) Emotional States
b) Mind Wandering
c) Skeptical Doubt
d) Brain Alertness
e) Focus & Neuro-Science

a)Emotional States: Emotional states and their effects are examples of psychological reasons interfering with focus.

Negative as well as positive emotional states have an impact on our ability to concentrate. Let's dig a little deeper to better understand it by looking at the various emotional states.

Negative Emotional State: The negative emotional state's negative influence on our ability to focus or work with our mental or intellectual faculties is revealed by functional brain imaging. As the mind is approached by an external threat, critical thinking, problem-solving, and creative thinking become more challenging in a negative emotional state. Negative emotions distort the pattern of attention on an item, task, or event.

Hate for something or someone can trigger negative emotions. For example, consider the following scenario- you're climbing a mountain, it starts to rain, the road is bumpy, and you have to swim. These are the tasks you dislike that cause unpleasant emotions and feelings, preventing you from focusing on your job and progressing.

Dr. Amy Arnsten is a Yale University Professor of Neuroscience and Psychology who focuses on the brain's response to stress. She's spent her career studying the brain's higher functions and how different arousal systems influence them – and, more precisely, how they might break down when confronted with certain stimuli. According to her research, our brain's prefrontal cortex (a chunk behind our forehead) conducts "higher functions," including critical thinking, impulse inhibition, and, most importantly, the ability to focus. Stress signaling weakens the prefrontal cortex, whereas the stress hormones that accompany it boost the fundamental brain processes.

When confronted with acute physical danger, the prefrontal cortex switches off to allow the more primitive parts of your brain to take over — the portions that can respond swiftly and effectively to defend you. This process must have been a component of our origin and evolution to protect us in perilous conditions. This works effectively in dangerous situations because it alerts the body to take immediate action. Still, it has the opposite effect in cases demanding deep concentration and focus since it no longer permits the prefrontal brain to direct us.

We can see the implications of this phenomenon in the present pandemic, where we face a persistent but not acute threat. We are cutting off the part of our brain that helps us think beyond the primitive – for lengthy periods because it is an ongoing problem. Instead of dealing with the immediate danger and moving on, we are cutting off the part of our brain that helps us think beyond the primal. And our capacity to concentrate is severely harmed. According to Dr. Asnsten, three critical aspects make Covid-19 particularly effective at cutting off our prefrontal cortex: its invisibility, the lack of individual control we have over it, and being forced to go against our typical routines to protect ourselves.

Before we were born, evolution built into the brain's signaling system taught it to respond to danger. This causes difficulty in focusing as well as a general lack of motivation. The "freeze" response is a part of our flight or fight response to danger, and it can seem a lot like mental paralysis. These primitive reactions can be connected to losing the ability to have genuinely motivated, guided behavior.

This results in a vicious cycle of losing attention, self-deprecation, and further deterioration of prefrontal connections for many people. Knowing this allows us to be gentle to ourselves and acknowledges that this is a natural aspect of our development. Once we recognize this, we can lower stress and break the cycle, reversing the cause and changing the outcome.

Positive Emotional State: Positive or high adrenalin states have a similar influence on focus as negative emotional states. For example, when we receive excellent news and are ecstatic, our adrenaline levels rise to dangerously high, leading to worry and poor work performance. This phenomenon is also known as the **Yerkes-Dodson Law**, which claims an optimum level of arousal for getting things done.

An exhilarating event pushes you much above your ideal level, making it difficult to concentrate. Carrying forward with our earlier example, consider the situation where you begin your journey towards scaling the mountain and, after climbing a mile, you come upon a restaurant. You are mesmerized by the atmosphere, the fragrance of the food, and the appearance of the people surrounding you. You experience pleasurable feelings and become stimulated. You become so enthralled that after a while, you abandon your upward trip and opt to stay put. This is an instance of a positive emotional state interfering with focus and causing distraction. This phenomenon is also referred to as a **sensory pleasure fixation**.

In a high or good emotional state, the focus continues shifting from one event to the next. For example, assume you've just got word of your promotion and raise. If you're asked to produce a critical report right after you've been told you've been promoted, it'll not be easy to concentrate. You're simply too pumped up, and your heightened emotional state makes even the most mundane activities nearly impossible to complete.

It is actually pretty simple to assess the impact of both low and high emotional states in our daily lives, as well as the consequences. Talking about myself, I can share, when I experience emotions like anger, concern, or despair, it is tough for me to concentrate and engage in a critical activity. Fear, worry, and stress arise due to such feelings, leaving me in a condition of inaction. Similarly, when I am incredibly joyful, excited, or in a state of complete euphoria, it becomes progressively difficult for me to concentrate.

b)Mind Wandering: It is natural for the mind to wander regularly. According to neuroscience, when we focus, we usually walk off into a world where our minds go in the opposite direction. A stray thought or emotion that may have surfaced in the mind field leads the brain to defocus. The posterior cingulate cortex, precuneus, and other brain parts surrounding the limbic system become more active, contributing to the distraction network. We may not even be aware of it at times. So, though we may be attempting to focus on something, our minds may be wandering off to an imaginary realm, wholly detached from the task at hand.

Excessive mind wandering generates tension and diverts focus away from critical tasks. It also prevents you from relaxing and being in the present moment. You can find it difficult to sleep because you miss the magnificent rainbow, the breeze, and the gentle music playing in the background.

Harvard researchers discovered that the human mind wanders 47% of the time. Over several days, 2,200 people from all over the world were randomly contacted and asked to use their iPhone to report what they were doing, thinking about, and feeling. Almost half of them were mentally absent while doing things like grooming, commuting, cooking, working, walking, shopping, and so on. According to the findings, when your mind wanders, you become more worried and dissatisfied than when you stay in the present moment. Furthermore, people were happier when they were focused on the action rather than allowing their minds to wander and think about anything else, regardless of whether they worked overtime, vacuuming the home, or were simply stuck in traffic.

MRI scanning investigations have also revealed that our brains wander even when we rest and think nothing. Numerous parts of the brain regulate this rest mode activity. This phenomenon is known as the brain's **default mode**

network. When there is no external disturbance, the brain switches to its default mode and activates the network. When there is an inflow of information from the outside, it logs out of the default mode.

The brain's calibration for arousal at an optimal level is one of the likely reasons for this phenomenon of brain tuning out regularly and in such opposing conditions. That's why, if the activity is tedious, monotonous, and can be completed on autopilot (like driving, vacuuming, other mundane tasks, or simply doing nothing), the brain seeks an exciting alternative on its own to keep us engaged and sends us wandering. We begin time travel through the past, present, and future as we hunt for something more thrilling, interesting, and engaging. There is less emphasis on the current state but more on the past and future. Spending more time in the past (which can't be altered) and tomorrow (which can't be controlled) produces negative emotions of worry, anxiety, and fear and makes it difficult to concentrate.

Neuroscientists at the University of California, Berkeley, discovered that we have various thoughts running through our heads, including stray, deliberately constrained, confined, and task-related ideas. The electrophysical characteristic of each type is distinct. These distinct signatures can aid in determining whether or not thoughts are wandering. So, you can tell if your thoughts are wandering or if you're concentrating. This wandering of the mind impairs concentration, causes errors, and makes it harder to make decisions.

c)Skeptical Doubt: At the beginning of my career, I worked in a position that required me to sell things directly to clients(business to customer model). I was a dismal failure at it. Later, I worked in another job involving channel sales. Here I was required to build a distribution network, create teams, appoint sales channels, which were supposed to sell to customers. I excelled in this job and performed exceptionally well. Unfortunately, I formed the impression in my head that I am not good at direct sales and should avoid it. As a result, whenever I came across an activity that needed me to do anything that resembled direct sales, I avoided it. In hindsight, I feel that perhaps I would have missed out on some really great opportunities in the process due to this self-doubt.

Skeptical doubt is a state of mind, which is related to indecision. When in this state, we get several questions in our mind:

- Can I do that?
- Should I that?
- What will others say?
- Am I good enough?
- I tried earlier, but it didn't work out
- The thing is not meant for me.
- Maybe someone else but not me
- I Will do it later
- Is it worth it?

And there is a slew of other similar questions that lead to self-doubt. When we allow such thoughts to play tricks in our minds, we enter a skeptical state. The emphasis turns to all of the reasons why we shouldn't do anything. It's akin to putting a query into the Google search field.

The search engine algorithm scans the database when we type a keyword and returns the results with the closest match. These self-doubt phrases serve as keywords for the brain, which then analyzes the database by scanning past occurrences. The instances that are the most similar to the thoughts that are passing through our heads are displayed on our brain's screen. This entire activity diverts attention away from the current task, resulting in inaction.

d)Brain Alertness: The levels of mental attentiveness in the brain fluctuate throughout the day. For example, early birds are most productive in the mornings when it is convenient to concentrate and focus on things. Similarly, night owls are most effective during the late hours of the day, when their bio clock and natural body rhythms are in sync. When we attempt deliberately or are forced to perform high-focus work at times that are not in sync with our natural rhythms, the problem occurs.

Sleep is a crucial element impacting the brain's alertness levels. According to a study from the University of Pennsylvania School of Medicine, sleep deprivation is linked to reduced cognitive performance, including working memory and speed. It also affects executive and alert attention. In addition, sleep deprivation for an extended period has been linked to the death of brain cells. According to a study published in The Journal of Neuroscience, mice were subjected to a sleep deprivation experiment. It was observed that LCns (locus ceruleus neurons) required for brain awareness were steadily disappearing.

LCns are essential for the brain's alertness. What's even scary is that a lack of sleep for an extended period may cause your brain cells to die. Regular neuronal output, combined with insufficient rest, led to their deterioration and eventual destruction. Within three days of the trial, the mice had lost 25% of their LCns, despite their sleep being limited to 4-5 hours. The findings of the study are directly applicable to human brains. It was essentially stating that a lack of sleep can cause the brain to die.

It's been my personal experience that on days when I have to sacrifice my daily sleep due to travel, work, or other obligations, it's challenging to concentrate on the simplest of tasks.

e) Focus & Neuroscience: Focus is concentrated attention; however, our attention can include several things simultaneously. One of the reasons restricting the ability to focus has its roots in our inherent ability to fix the attention on all but one thing.

Switching from one task to the next necessitates the use of our prefrontal brain (PFC). Because this part of the brain loves novelty, new stimuli trigger the release of reward chemicals like dopamine (similar to the feeling we get when we eat something yummy). Every time you check a notification, email, social media, etc., these feel-good hormones are released into your brain's pleasure centers. As a result, it feels nice to engage in diversions. Furthermore, the brain region that is stimulated when we are concentrated craves novelty.

This makes it difficult to focus on one thing at a time and encourages you to engage in diversions or finish a large number of small/insignificant chores (such as checking email) rather than larger/more concentrate-demanding chores.

What are some of the costs of doing numerous jobs at the same time?

1.Both psychologically and physically exhausts us.

- It can have a long-term harmful effect on our brains!
- It uses more glucose, making us fatigued and confused.
- Cortisol and adrenaline levels rise as a result of this.

2. We slow down.

- It takes a fraction of a second to move from one task to another.
- This expense can cause you to take 40% longer to do the identical tasks as if you did them individually.

3.We make more errors.

- Our short-term memory is harmed.
- Our working IQ can be reduced by 10-15 points!

Understanding Attention

Our brains are constantly bombarded with sensory data from the outside world. As a result, the brain's ability to comprehend information effectively on a moment-by-moment basis is restricted. The brain overcomes this stumbling block by devising a system for prioritizing information flow. It's the brain's inherent method for concentrating upon the most critical information and ignoring the rest. "**Attention**" is the process through which the brain accomplishes this.

When it comes to focus and attention, two brain systems are at work, and the way they interact influences our capacity to focus on a task. Primarily, there are two types of attention:

Top-Down Attention: "Top-down" attention – also known as **endogenous attention** – occurs when the brain dictates and instructs how and where you should focus your attention. The brain decides based on what you were trying to accomplish and prior information and experience from memory. The neocortex, which is a relatively newer part of the brain, is responsible for endogenous attention. It is the brain's source of voluntary control and aids in the concentration of our thoughts while screening out distractions. "It adds capabilities like self-awareness and reflection, deliberation and planning to our mind's repertoire," says Daniel Goleman, a psychologist and author of the best-selling book Emotional Intelligence.

Bottom-up Attention: Attention is considered **"bottom-up" or exogenous attention** when driven by the sensory world. Bottom-up attentional processing is carried out by the older, more primitive region of the brain. This form of processing is impulsive and reactive. It monitors input guided by our senses - it is our warning system, usually triggered by negative emotions like dread. Not only that, but the alerts generated by this system are often difficult to dismiss.

Consider the following situation: Assume you're strolling down a crowded street. There is a variety of merchandise on display. A vast array of things, begging for your attention. Colors, forms, and sounds all appeal to you. The scenario in which the loudest voice or the brightest color "wins," causing you to refocus your attention, describes the bottoms-up attention. As we go about our daily lives, both systems are at work, defining our attention.

The attention system in the brain assists in switching focus back and forth as needed. When multitasking, it also allows for the split of attention between two things at the same time. Sometimes we need to focus our attention for a brief time, while other times, we need to retain it longer.

Mental focus is the ability to concentrate on a specific goal or task while shutting out distracting sounds for an extended length of time. When we try to focus, we don't even recognize the process in our subconscious minds. When we try to focus on anything or seek something, we are most aware of the object or task in our focus. Still, our brain pays attention to many materials, related or unrelated, on a millisecond basis. Even the act of walking requires the brain to pay attention to the ground contours and the positioning of each foot.

There are three sorts of attention that have an impact on our ability to concentrate:

I. **Selective attention**: Paying attention to one item while neglecting others. Focusing on work in a coffee shop while ignoring discussions around you is an example of this.

II. **Multitasking:** Managing attention between numerous tasks simultaneously (attention switching). Driving your car is an illustration of this.

III. **Sustained attention**: The act of focusing on one subject for an extended period (while ignoring distractions). Playing a video game is an example of this.

Because there are so many different types of attention, the reasons for their genesis have been thoroughly researched. According to research, the two most severe types of attention are the most restrictive. Tunnel vision occurs when we are overly attentive, and the mind narrows as a result. On the other hand, when we don't pay attention, we lose control of our thoughts and become scatter-brained.

Distraction is a finely calibrated feature of our brains, and for a good reason. From an evolutionary standpoint, it has been critical for our survival that our brains filter out a massive amount of information so that we may focus on something potentially life-threatening. We needed to be quickly distracted to be aware of any hazards approaching us.

In the brain, there is no single "attention center." Instead, the ability to focus attention relies on a vast network of brain regions that make up the brain's attentional system. This system works closely with our thoughts, actions, emotions, and feelings to improve their efficiency. This network's activation promotes attentional and mental focus.

The attentional system is made up of areas in each of the brain's lobes. The information being attended to and how the attention is directed determine the activation of specific regions. The core attentional network comprises sensory areas that selectively process the incoming information-parietal regions, which control and decide the focus areas, and prefrontal regions that form the attentional control center (upper part for top-down attention and lower for bottom-up attention).

Attention and focus are aided by neuromodulators such as acetylcholine, dopamine, and norepinephrine. They are crucial in guaranteeing adequate attention concentration wherever required in the face of undesirable distractions vying for the brain's resources.

- **Acetylcholine:** Acetylcholine (ACh) is a neurochemical that helps people pay attention, learn, and remember things. ACh cells made up of nuclei from our evolutionarily older brainstem, and midbrain may be found in almost every part of the brain. Ach improves attentional concentration by regulating neuronal activity in the brain's sensory, prefrontal, and parietal areas. In addition, it enhances the signal in sensory regions like the visual cortex that are connected to noise. Simply said, the higher the noise from the source, the stronger the relevant brain signal, which determines the focus point. This enables detecting the most pertinent portions of the visual field and suppressing surrounding distractions that may otherwise divert attention.

  By modulating both top-down (brain-driven) and bottom-up (sensation-driven) attentional processes in the parietal cortex, ACh supports the way we orient and redirect our attention towards something of interest or importance.

- **Dopamine:** Even though dopamine activities in the brain are complex, experimental investigations have demonstrated that it aids in enhancing attention, particularly in the context of ensuring that we pay attention and move our focus flexibly and suitably based on previously learned information. To put it another way, knowing what to concentrate on when utilizing the experience. If we cannot do so, we will waste a significant amount of time examining useless data. Dopamine aids your attention efficiency in a dynamic and ever-changing environment in this way. In addition, it aids in balancing and fine-tuning the overall pattern of brain activity to suit the situation.

- **Norepinephrine:** The neurotransmitter norepinephrine is located in the brain (adrenaline). It's a neurotransmitter that plays a role in wakefulness, memory, awareness, and generally preparing the brain (and thus the body) for action when challenged or threatened. In the brain, norepinephrine has various activities that activate and inhibit specific brain areas.

  It acts on systems that enable arousal - or mental vigilance - and wakefulness, one of its primary tasks. It stimulates ACh cells that promote wakefulness and inhibits GABAergic cells that encourage sleep. Increases in brain arousal, or alertness, are associated with gains in cognitive functioning, such as attentional focus and reaction times.

  Norepinephrine is vital in mediating the attention effect when your attention is suddenly "grabbed" by an unexpected, novel, or significant stimulus or event that occurs or appears in your surroundings, in addition to its overall role of alertness and alertness.

- **Noradrenaline**: It works in the brain through two types of receptors: alpha and beta. The medial prefrontal cortex, the anterior cingulate cortex - an area involved in mental flexibility - and your motor cortex, which governs movement planning and execution, are connected to the locus coeruleus differently.

"If we want to devote our complete concentration, something happens in the brain to enable us to focus and filter out distractions," says Professor Stephen Williams of the Queensland Brain Institute at UQ.

Studies have demonstrated that the brain's electrical activity changes when we focus our attention. Neurons stop communicating with one another and begin firing out of synchrony. This is advantageous because it permits individual neurons to react to sensory information in a variety of ways. As a result, we can concentrate on a car rushing down the road or a conversation with a buddy in a busy room.

The cholinergic system in the brain is responsible for causing this desynchronization. The system comprises clusters of specific neurons that synthesize and release acetylcholine, a signaling molecule, and these clusters form extensive connections throughout the brain. This cholinergic system not only acts as a master switch but accumulating evidence suggests it also allows the brain to determine which sensory input is the most salient — i.e., deserving of attention — at any given time and then focus on that input.

It sends a message to the brain about what is vital to be aware of. The cholinergic system is thought to have a wide range of effects on our cognitive abilities. Its obliteration impairs cognition and memory formation. Progressive deterioration of the procedure happens in humans in conditions like Alzheimer's disease, which impairs cognition and memory.

It has been discovered that when we are focused on something specific, the emission of neurons in the visual cortex relating to the object we are focusing on speeds up. At the same time, those reacting to irrelevant information are repressed.

The activity of neurons in the visual cortex is synchronized when they oscillate at the same frequency. When it comes to attention and focus vs. inattention and distraction, the frequency of oscillation is crucial. Increased synchrony between neurons in the alpha range (8–12 Hz) has been linked to inattention and distracting information in humans. Increased gamma synchrony (approximately 30-150 Hz) has been related to attention and focus on a target.

According to neuroscience, the prefrontal cortex, namely the dorsal prefrontal cortex, is active when we focus on anything. This area collaborates with other brain areas to create the executive control network, a regional network. This network uses working memory and cognitive flexibility. All brain parts are activated when we concentrate, with the dorsal prefrontal cortex playing a pivotal role. This part of the prefrontal cortex can also suppress information that we aren't interested in and limit our sensory data.

There is no doubt that the brain & psychology plays a vital role in focus. But, after the brain, it's our body that influences concentration ability. So, let's find out how?

2) Physiology of Focus(State of Body): This encompasses our body's general physical well-being and functionality. It includes elements such as energy levels: low energy levels make it difficult to concentrate. As we know, all of our bodily functions require energy. Routine activities, or rather non-critical jobs, typically consume the greatest energy. It's too much to hope for increased concentration while you're running low on fuel.

There is a direct correlation between physical & mental well-being. Focus is primarily the brain's function; hence, the state of physical health indirectly affects the ability to concentrate and focus. Several hypotheses have been proposed in an attempt to figure out how physical activity affects mental health. Let's understand how physical health impacts the functioning of our mind and mental health.

Being unable to concentrate and focus can be the result of chronic health conditions, as under:

a) Alcohol use disorder

b) Attention deficit hyperactivity disorder (ADHD)

c) Chronic fatigue syndrome

d) Concussion

e) Dementia

f) Epilepsy

g) Insomnia

h) Depression

i) Anxiety

a)Alcohol use disorder: When you drink too much alcohol, chemical changes in the brain occur, and you develop an alcohol use disorder. These modifications make you feel more enjoyable. This encourages you to drink more frequently, even if it is harmful. Unfortunately, the pleasurable feelings connected with alcohol consumption fade over time, and a person with an alcohol use problem will continue to drink to avoid withdrawal symptoms.

These withdrawal symptoms can be unpleasant and perhaps dangerous. When you stop drinking, you may experience withdrawal symptoms such as shaking, nausea, vomiting, blacking out & memory lapses. This condition causes disorientation of the brain, making it increasingly difficult to concentrate and focus. We all have experienced the ill effects of alcoholism around us. Many fatal accidents are an outcome of alcohol consumption by drivers.

b)Attention deficit hyperactivity disorder (ADHD): Attention deficit hyperactivity disorder (ADHD) is a mental health condition that causes excessive hyperactivity and impulsivity. People with ADHD may also have difficulty concentrating on a single task or remaining motionless for long periods. Both adults and children can have ADHD. The American Psychiatric Association (APA) acknowledges this diagnosis. ADHD is linked to a wide range of behaviors. The following are a few of the more common ones:

- having difficulty concentrating or focusing on tasks
- forgetfulness when it comes to finishing assignments
- being prone to distraction
- having a hard time staying still
- interrupting someone in the middle of a conversation

The American Psychological Association (APA) has divided ADHD into three forms to make diagnosis more consistent. These personalities are primarily inattentive, mostly hyperactive-impulsive, or a mixture of the two.

- **Predominantly inattentive:** People with this type of ADHD have a lot of trouble focusing, finishing work, and following instructions, as the name implies. Many children with inattentive ADHD, according to experts, may not receive a correct diagnosis because they do not disrupt the classroom. In addition, girls are more prone to have ADHD of this type.

- **Predominantly hyperactive- only impulsive type:** This kind of ADHD is characterized by hyperactive and impulsive conduct. Fidgeting, interrupting people while they're talking, and not waiting their turn are all examples of this. Although inattention is less of an issue with this form of ADHD, people with mainly hyperactive-impulsive ADHD may still struggle to concentrate on tasks.

- **Combined hyperactive-impulsive and inattentive type:** This is the most frequent attention deficit hyperactivity disorder (ADHD). In this kind of ADHD, people experience both inattentive and hyperactive symptoms. These include an inability to focus, a penchant for impulsivity, and higher-than-normal activity and energy levels.

Causes of ADHD

Despite the prevalence of ADHD, doctors and academics are still baffled as to what causes it. It's thought to have neurological roots. However, genetics could also be a factor. According to research, dopamine deficiency is a component of ADHD. Dopamine is a brain molecule that aids in the transmission of signals from one nerve to another. It aids in the elicitation of emotional responses and motions. According to other studies, there is a structural difference in the brain. According to the findings, those with ADHD had a lower grey matter volume. The brain's grey matter comprises sections that help with speech, self-control, decision making, & muscle control.

c)Chronic fatigue syndrome: Chronic fatigue syndrome (CFS) is characterized by extreme weariness or exhaustion that does not go away with rest and is not caused by medical disease. CFS's causes aren't entirely understood. Viral infection, psychological stress, or a mix of variables are some of the possibilities. CFS can affect anybody, but it is most frequent in women in their 40s and. Although there is presently no cure, medication can help to alleviate symptoms.

According to researchers, some of the major causes for this condition include a compromised immune system, anxiety, and hormonal inconsistencies.CFS can also cause sleep disturbances, such as after a night's sleep, feeling unrefreshed. It can also cause insomnia, loss of memory, and reduced concentration.

d)Concussion: A mild traumatic brain injury(TBI) is known as a concussion. It can happen after a head injury or a whiplash-type injury that causes your head and brain to shake back and forth quickly. A concussion causes a change in mental state, which may include unconsciousness. A fall, a car collision, or any other regular activity can cause injury to anyone. However, you have a higher chance of developing a concussion if you participate in high-impact sports like football or boxing. Concussions are rarely fatal, but they can induce severe symptoms that necessitate medical attention.

The signs of a concussion may include:

- memory problems
- confusion
- drowsiness or feeling sluggish
- dizziness
- double vision or blurred vision
- headache
- nausea or vomiting
- sensitivity to light or noise
- balance problems
- slowed reaction to stimuli

The symptoms may begin immediately, or they may not develop for hours, days, weeks, or even months following your injury. During the recovery period after a concussion, you may experience the following symptoms:

- irritability
- sensitivity to light or noise
- difficulty concentrating

- mild headaches

e)Dementia: A loss of cognitive function characterizes dementia. The mental impairment must affect at least two brain functions to be classified as dementia. Dementia can have an impact on memory, thinking, language, judgment, behavior. In its early stages, dementia can cause symptoms, such as:

- **Resistance to change:** You may have a hard time accepting changes in schedules or the environment.

- **Reduced memory retention:** You or a loved one can remember the events of 15 years ago like it was yesterday, but you can't remember what you had for lunch.

- **Reaching for the right words:** Word recollection or association may be more difficult.

- **Repetition:** You may ask the same question, complete the same task, or tell the same story multiple times.

- **Low sense of direction:** Places you once knew well may now feel foreign. You may also struggle with driving routes you've taken for years because it no longer looks familiar.

- **Attention issues:** You may find following a person's story or description complex.

- **Mood Swings:** Depression, frustration, and anger are not uncommon for people with dementia.

- **Boredom:** Apathy may occur in people with dementia. This includes losing interest in hobbies or activities that you once enjoyed.

- **Lack of familiarity**: People, places, and events may no longer feel familiar. You might not remember people who know you.

- **Easy tasks becoming tough:** You may struggle to recall how to do jobs you've done for many years.

A variety of factors can cause dementia. It is caused by the degeneration of neurons (brain cells) or changes in other body systems that impair the function of neurons.

f)Epilepsy: Epilepsy is a chronic condition that produces recurring, spontaneous seizures. A seizure is a burst of electrical activity in the brain that occurs suddenly. Seizures can be divided into two categories:

#Seizures that impact the entire brain are known as **generalized seizures**.

#**Focal seizures**, also known as partial seizures, affect only one portion of the brain. As a result, it can be challenging to spot a minor seizure. It can last a few seconds, and you won't be aware of it.

More severe seizures can produce muscle spasms and involuntary cramps, and they can last anywhere from a few seconds to several minutes. Some people become disoriented or lose consciousness after a stronger seizure. You may have no recollection of what happened afterward. There are several reasons you might have a seizure. These include high fever, head trauma, very low blood sugar, alcohol withdrawal.

A few of the most commonly reported triggers are lack of sleep, illness or fever, stress, bright lights, flashing lights or patterns, caffeine, alcohol, medicines, or drugs, skipping meals, overeating, or specific food ingredients.

g)Insomnia: Insomnia is a form of sleep deprivation. Insomniacs have trouble falling asleep, staying asleep, or doing both. When people with insomnia get up from their sleep, they typically do not feel refreshed. Fatigue and other symptoms may result as a result of this. According to the American Psychological Association, almost one-third of all individuals experience insomnia symptoms. Approximately 6 to 10% of all individuals have symptoms severe enough to be diagnosed with insomnia disorder.

The causes of your insomnia will depend on the type of sleeplessness you experience. Short-term insomnia, or acute insomnia, may be caused by several things, including stress, an upsetting or traumatic event, changes to your sleep habits, like sleeping in a hotel or new home, physical pain, jet lag, certain medications.

Chronic insomnia lasts for at least three months and can be primary or secondary. Primary insomnia has no known cause. Secondary insomnia occurs with another condition that can include:

- medical conditions that make it harder to sleep, such as arthritis or back pain
- psychological issues, such as anxiety or depression
- substance use
- sleep apnea
- diabetes

h)Depression: Feeling down, sad, or upset is normal. It can be concerning feeling that way for several days or weeks on end. Physical symptoms and behavioral changes caused by depression include:

- decreased energy, chronic fatigue, or feeling sluggish frequently
- difficulty concentrating, making decisions, or recalling
- pain, aches, cramps, or gastrointestinal problems without any apparent cause
- changes in appetite or weight
- difficulty in sleeping, waking early or oversleeping

Emotional symptoms of depression include:

- loss of interest or no longer finding pleasure in activities or hobbies
- persistent feelings of sadness, anxiety, or emptiness
- feeling hopeless or pessimistic
- anger, irritability, or restlessness
- feeling guilty or experiencing feelings of worthlessness or helplessness
- thoughts of death or suicide
- suicide attempts

i)Anxiety: Anxiety, or fear and worry, can happen to anyone from time to time, too. It's not unusual to experience anxiety before a big event or important decision. But chronic stress can be debilitating and lead to irrational thoughts and fears that interfere with your daily life. Physical symptoms and behavioral changes caused by generalized anxiety disorder include feeling fatigued quickly, difficulty concentrating or recalling, muscle tension, racing heart, grinding teeth, sleep difficulties, including problems falling asleep and restless, unsatisfying sleep.

Anxiety's emotional symptoms include restlessness, irritability, feeling on edge, difficulty controlling worry or fear, dread, and panic.

This concludes, coverage of internal state factors having a bearing on our concentration and focus levels. In my view, save for exceptional medical conditions, it is relatively easy to control them. Thus, we can take care of our body and mind so that focusing becomes more effortless.

We will extensively cover the external environment elements and their impact on our focus in the next step. However, before we move forward, a small caveat, controlling external factors may not be possible in all situations, yet we can manage them.

External State Factors

Essentially, it comprises the external environment, surroundings, people, place, and other elements, which play a crucial role in enabling or disabling focus. Since the origin of these factors is tagged into the outside world or external environment, these are slightly less controllable.

According to Rachelle Scott, MD, medical director of psychiatry at Eden Health, "Our environment is a combination of both physical variables such as where we live and the people around us both in your home but also on a larger community scale." As a result, what we see, hear, inhale, and smell can impact our mood and stress levels, directly affecting our mental health and, therefore, focus. For example, bright light can help with despair and anxiety, especially amid the long winter days.

Loud noises and big crowds can be overpowering, causing cortisol levels to rise and stress levels to rise. Pollution has an impact on mental health as well. Shreds of evidence suggest more polluted places have a higher incidence of depression. In addition, the influence of mold in the household and higher asthma rates resulting from increased pollutants can potentially cause mental health issues.

Practically, anything in your environment can affect your mental health. The broad categorization of these elements can be done as under:

1.**Aesthetics:** The ambiance of the place aids focus, while cluttered spaces might make us feel overwhelmed and anxious. Conventionally, authors and writers have come out of their best works while functioning from scenic locations with amazing aesthetics.

2.**Sensory:** An environment's lighting, temperature, sounds, smells, and color palette are essential factors in how comfortable, relaxed, and safe we feel. Harsh lighting and loud noises, for example, might cause anxiety or agitation, while dark and cold settings, especially in the winter, can make us feel unmotivated.

3.**People:** The kind of people we are surrounded by plays a critical role in directing the focus & quality of output. The right type of people with similar habits and objectives complement the work and vice versa. Managing ineffective or inconsistent communication, disagreements, or untrustworthy people in the workplace can be highly stressful.

4.**Culture & Values:** Cultural fit and harmonization of values are essential for mental well-being. Non-alignment or conflicting behaviors create friction, which generates negative emotions like stress, anxiety, and worry. People must interact with individuals who share their culture and values to be understood on a deeper level. If not, feelings of isolation and depression may develop. These emotions cloud the ability to reason and work with the required focus.

5.Familiarity: Uncertainty prompts sentiments like anxiousness. If something in the environment, such as a problematic relationship or disorganization, reminds us of a terrible time, it shifts the concentration from the present work to past events. Positive associations in the environment, such as a family heirloom, images, or familiar objects, might, on the other hand, improve mood and sense of connection. A relaxed mind helps in amplifying concentration by letting us remain in the present.

With all its elements, the external environment becomes a potent source of distractions, trying its best to deviate us from the object of our attention.

Understanding Distraction

As per Merriam-Webster dictionary, a **distraction** is" a thing that prevents someone from giving full attention to something else." The inability to pay attention, a lack of interest in the object of focus, or the tremendous intensity, novelty, or attractiveness of something other than the object of obsession are all causes of distraction. Visual stimuli, social encounters, music, text messages, and phone calls are all external distractions. Hunger, exhaustion, illness, stress, and daydreaming are examples of internal distractions. Distractions from both the outside and the inside lead to the loss of focus.

Simply put, distraction isn't about being unable to concentrate; it's about allowing yourself to become preoccupied with something other than the activity at hand. This is infuriating because it causes tasks to take significantly longer than they should. Because our brain is always scrambling to reposition itself, it has the exact switching costs of multitasking when it happens frequently. Notice how quickly we can find anything else to do whenever your project becomes difficult? This is because distractions provide brief respites from discomfort. That fast Instagram scroll is like a stress reliever at the end of a long day. Distraction concerns predate the internet era as well. People have struggled with distractions such as TV and radios & other technologies earlier.

We lose productivity and energy as a result of distractions. They impact our ability to concentrate and persist with projects or jobs long enough to complete them.

The environment outside us poses myriad challenges and offers distractions galore.

When we try to concentrate these days, it seems virtually hard not to be distracted. Our phones and computers have become an integral part of our lives that the internet, app notifications, and other distractions are nearly impossible to escape.

Even if we get past the first layer of electronic/social media distraction, we'll still be distracted by other people and outdoor noise, making it tough to concentrate.

Our thoughts and feelings, which seem to wander much of the time aimlessly, are also included as distractions.

A 2016 survey of 2,000 US hiring and HR managers by CareerBuilder showed that the top distraction culprits included smartphones (55%), the internet (41%), gossip (37%), social media (37%), co-workers dropping by (27%), smoking or snack breaks (27%), email (26%), meetings, (24%), and noisy co-workers (20%).

The top 12 external environment distractions at the workplace can be summarized as under:

1.Office colleagues: At work, it's critical to cultivate relationships with your team and co-workers. Daily interactions are essential for fostering a friendly, collaborative attitude and mood in the workplace, yet it's easy to become engrossed in endless chitchat and gossip.

If our office door is always open, it's pretty easy for someone to come in and ask you a question, which draws you away from your work.

2.Noisy work Environment: According to research conducted by Kim and de Dear at the University of Sydney, 30% of workers in cubicles and roughly 25% of workers in open-plan offices are unhappy with noise levels at work.

According to Ipsos and Steelcase's Workspace Futures Team, 85 percent of people are unsatisfied with their working environment and cannot concentrate. In addition, 95% of those polled stated working quietly was vital to them, yet just 41% claimed they could do so, and 31% said they had to leave the office to do their work.

If you work in a large or small workplace, you've probably seen that noise levels may quickly rise, whether it's from discussions, phone calls, music, or other sources.

3.Emails: "Limit email consumption and production," says Tim Ferriss, "because it is the largest single interruption in the modern world."

We're all aware of how inconvenient e-mail can be.

You're working on a critical project when you get an e-mail indicating that you've received a message.

You now have two options-You can either leave what you're doing to read the email, or you can stay on task and read the email later.

Many people spend their entire day in this manner. They're entirely focused on completing a critical task when an email notice arrives. You put down what you're doing, go to your inbox, and read the email, which is often utterly unrelated and has no bearing on your current priorities.

These emails can create a constant sense of bustle, and, as a result, many projects are left incomplete at the end of the day. As a result, we may feel as if we haven't had a particularly productive day.

4.Mobile Phones: Constantly staring at your phone disrupts your workflow and concentration.

According to Deloitte's recent research, the average consumer checks their smartphone 47 times a day. So if you check your phone an average of 47 times per day and work an 8-hour day, you may be checking it nearly six times each hour. That would be enough to divert anyone's attention.

Smartphones and other devices, as we all know, regularly interrupt us and divert our focus away from the project or activity at hand.

It's all too easy to get distracted from our vital jobs to check our phones, watches, and other electronic devices.

5.Social Media: The favorite punching bag for productivity geeks, and rightly so. Instagram, Linked In, Twitter, Facebook, YouTube, and Pinterest, to name a few. The number of apps and websites vying for our attention is practically limitless. Likewise, there is an endless supply of knowledge available to us from our friends, co-workers, news channels, and businesses. As you are reading this, some of your co-workers are presumably checking their social media accounts. In modern times, social media applications have emerged as one of the prominent sources of distractions.

6.Meetings: Meetings are essential for brainstorming ideas, arriving at the action plan, execution, and review. Just like technology and other enablers, overexploitation has made the boon into a bane. Meetings, for the heck of it, at best serve as a source of distraction. Over the last year, the changing work environment, where virtual meetings have replaced physical ones, has worsened the situation. No one wants to squander an hour or two in an ineffective meeting during a hectic week.

I'm sure many of you would respond to "poor meetings" if I asked you the most effective method to be inefficient. Meetings now take up more time than ever before. As per studies, the average employee attends 62 meetings every month, but half are deemed ineffective.

According to some estimates, employees spend 31 hours in unproductive meetings over a month, with 91% admitting to daydreaming and 39% admitting to falling asleep.

7. Multi-tasking: Most of us have developed a habit of multitasking. Without a doubt, it's stressful, but we've trained our brains to be unfocused. When we're anxious, the amygdala sends a stress signal to the hypothalamus, which tells the adrenal glands that we're under a lot of strain. Your adrenal glands react by releasing adrenaline into your system.

As shared in the earlier section, too much adrenaline causes excessive arousal, making it even more challenging to concentrate and execute. It may seem simple to tell ourselves that we will focus on only one thing at a time, but you realize how difficult it may be when you do it. When you resist the impulse to multitask and set your mind to focusing on only one activity at a time, external events and workplace surroundings often force you to do so. In either case, the purpose is defeated.

8.Messy workplace: While a bit of clutter can inspire creativity in tiny quantities, the reality remains that a messy workspace impairs your capacity to focus and process information—confusion and disarray act as a to-do list, reminding you of all that has to be done. As a result, it drags you away from the current moment. This makes you increasingly worried and stressed over time. By now, we already know stress reduces focus.

9.Excessive Supervision: Being a helicopter boss is simply a distraction for the employees. They find it aggravating, unsettling, and anxiety-inducing if managers constantly interrupt the team by stressing over every detail. Supervisors should instead encourage ownership and let them accomplish what they are supposed to do. Imagine being in the middle of a project model when your boss walks in and points out everything you did wrong. What percentage of your time do you believe you'll be productive? Disruptions are distractions that impede concentration, limit creativity, hamper personal development, and erode employee trust.

10.Comfort: The level of comfort might have an impact on your productivity. If you change into your nightgown, jump into bed, then turn on your laptop and start working, you might find yourself waking up from an unintended slumber a few hours later. You'll also fidget more than you'll learn if your position is overly unpleasant, such as sitting in a broken library chair. Make sure you're aware of how you're feeling; if your body feels too relaxed or you're comfortable enough to fall asleep, find another place to study.

Not only will working in uncomfortable position harm your posture, but it will also hinder your ability to concentrate. Studying in bed, for example, can cause you to toss and frequently turn and generate a stiff neck. If you want to learn, make sure you are in the most comfortable position possible. Do not accept a broken armchair, your carpet, or the bus as an option. If you're sitting at a proper desk, you'll be able to concentrate better on your studies or work.

11.Lighting: When trying to read something in dim light, straining your eyes makes it much more challenging to stay focused. To participate in a successful study, you must have adequate illumination to avoid headaches. Dim lighting can also make you feel more comfortable and make you want to crawl into bed, especially if you're close to one. So when you sit down to study or work, pay attention to the lighting in the room.

12.Temperature: Extreme temperatures, too hot or too cold, are detrimental to productivity. Warm temperatures make us sleepy, whereas chilly ones can make us feel uneasy. I have personally experienced it on my own & I see the change in output quality by adjusting the temperature.

The list of distractions in the external environment shared above might not be exhaustive, but these are the ones that come at the top of the table & contribute to the extent of 99%. If you observe closely and notice the things in your surroundings taking away your focus and attention, you would agree that more or less those fit into the ambit of these things only.

With this, we come to the end of this chapter. I am aware that this was a lengthy section, but it was necessary. Lack of focus or concentration is an effect. To change the outcome, knowledge of the causes is essential. Once we acquire a deep understanding of the causes, overcoming the obstructions becomes convenient by following the right approach.

I am sure you would be keenly looking forward to the 'How' part of the focus, which will be covered in the next chapter. So let's continue the journey.

Chapter 3:Synopsis

To understand why it is challenging to focus, we must understand the various elements impacting our concentration.

Broad classification of factors impacting focus:

- **Internal state factors:** Comprises of intrinsic elements and can be controlled at our end. These can be further subdivided into the state of mind(psychology) and state of the body(physiology).

- **Psychology of focus (State of Mind):** The guiding factors which determine the psychology of focus can be enumerated as under:

  a) Emotional states: Positive as well as negative emotional states are included in this:

  Negative emotional state: Low emotional state creates stress. Stress signaling weakens the prefrontal cortex, responsible for higher functions like critical thinking, impulse inhibition & the ability to focus. Fear, worry, anxiety are some causes of a negative emotional state.

  Positive emotional state: High emotional state increases the adrenaline levels above permissible levels, making it difficult to concentrate. Fixation to sensory pleasures like tasty food, pleasant environment, and physical appearance causes a positive emotional state, making it challenging to focus.

  Yerkes-Dodson Law: To have a good concentration, there has to be an optimum level of arousal. So, it essentially states that a balance between positive and negative emotional states is a must to focus and work efficiently.

b) Mind-wandering: The human mind wanders for approx.—50% of the time. While we may focus, the mind travels in the past and future instead of being present. The phenomenon is even more common for routine activities like walking and shopping that don't require extraordinary effort. As per the MRI scan studies, mind wandering happens even while we rest and do nothing. Various brain parts regulate this activity, and this phenomenon is known as the brain's default mode network.

Our brain is calibrated for arousal at the optimum level. If the activity is monotonous and boring, it tarts looking for exciting alternatives for engagement by traveling to the past or future. It starts looking for relief by searching the pleasurable activities in the mind stack if it is a highly complex task.
The excessive wandering of the mind causes tension and digresses attention from critical tasks. It also translates to excessive errors and poor decision-making.

c)Skeptical doubt: Self-doubt is a state of indecisiveness of mind. It is an outcome of negative thoughts. Negative thoughts give birth to negative emotions like stress, worry, anxiety, fear, and doubt. Negative emotions distract the mind from being focused on the present & cause inaction.

d)Brain alertness: Attentiveness of the brain varies during the day depending on the biological clock. The concentration levels reach the maximum depending on the natural rhythm of the body. Sleep plays a vital role in determining brain alertness levels—consistent sleep deprivation for long-duration damages the brain cells resulting in reduced cognitive performance. Lack of brain alertness makes the simplest of tasks challenging.

e) Focus & neuro-science

Attention: It is the process by which the brain concentrates on the most critical information and ignores the rest. There are two types of attention:

1.Top-down attention or Endogenous attention: It's a process where the brain guides and decides the object of attention. The focus of attention is decided basis the priority of work to be accomplished. The neocortex part of the brain drives endogenous attention.

2.Bottom-up attention or Exogenous attention: Our senses drive it. The strongest of senses compels the brain to determine the object of focus. The primitive brain is responsible for this function. For example, while in a crowded marketplace, the loudest of noise, strongest of smell, or the outlet's aesthetics attracts our attention.

Classification of attention, basis ability to concentrate:

1.Selective attention: Focused attention for a short period while ignoring distractions.

2.Multi-tasking: Shifting attention between multiple tasks.

3.Sustained attention: Selective attention for an extended duration.

Neuro Chemistry of attention

Neuromodulators that aid attention and focus are as under:

Acetylcholine (Ach): It helps in paying attention, learning, and memory retention.

Dopamine: It determines what to focus on based on past information. It provides the flexibility of focus by scanning the records.

Norepinephrine: This neurotransmitter is responsible for brain alertness. It stimulates brain arousal and restricts cells that promote sleep. Enhanced brain alertness alleviates cognitive functioning, focus, and reaction times.

Noradrenaline: Planning an execution is governed by this neurotransmitter.

- **Physiology of focus (State of Body)**: It covers the body's general well-being and its impact on focus.

Chronic health conditions responsible for lacking focus and concentration can be summarized as under:

a) Alcohol use disorder: Excessive intake of alcohol causes chemical changes in the brain. The alterations give you a feeling of pleasure while consuming alcohol. If you stop drinking, you experience withdrawal symptoms, leading to the disorientation of the brain, lack of concentration and focus.

b) Attention deficit hyperactivity disorder (ADHD): It's a mental health condition that causes hyperactivity and impulsivity. Sitting in one place and concentration on one task becomes difficult under this condition.

There are three types of ADHD

#Predominantly inattentive: Trouble in focusing, following instructions, and finishing work.
#Predominantly hyperactive: Fidgeting, interrupting people during conversation.
#Combined: Most common type, which is a combination of the above two conditions.

c)chronic fatigue syndrome: Extreme weariness and exhaustion of the body, which can't be cured by rest and result of any medical condition. It causes insomnia, memory loss, reduced brain alertness, and diminished concentration.

d)Concussion: It is also known as mild traumatic injury. An injury that causes the head and brain to shake back and forth rapidly causes a concussion. Accidents like car collisions, falling from a height may result in trauma. Memory problems, dizziness, blurred vision, headache, slow reaction, etc., are the effects.
e) Dementia: Loss of cognitive function signifies dementia. It is caused by the degeneration of neurons in the brain or changes in other body systems that impair the functioning of neurons. It impacts memory, thinking, behavior, judgment, frequent mood changes, difficulty in completing daily tasks.

f) Epilepsy: It causes seizures, which are sudden bursts of electrical activity in the brain. High fever, very low blood sugar, alcohol withdrawal symptom, etc., are the possible causes. Loss of consciousness and disorientation are the possible outcomes.

g) Insomnia: It is the condition of sleep deprivation for long durations.

Acute or short-term insomnia: Stress, traumatic events, changes in sleeping habits, sleeping place. Certain medical conditions, jet lag, etc.

Chronic Insomnia: Lasts for three months and above. Causes include medical conditions like arthritis or back pain, psychological issues-anxiety or depression, substance abuse, diabetes, etc.
Outcomes: Fatigue, not feeling fresh, reduced brain alertness, lack of concentration.

h) Depression: Feeling of sadness and upset for extended duration classifies depression. Causes include loss of interest, anxiety, sadness, hopelessness, pessimism, anger, irritation, restlessness, etc.
Outcomes: Reduced energy, chronic fatigue, lack of concentration, poor decision making, memory loss, etc.

i)Anxiety: It can happen to anyone for any reason, such as before a big event or an important decision. However, anxiety for a prolonged duration causes restlessness, fear, panic, dread, and irritability.

❖ **External state Factors:** The broad categorization of external factors can be done as under:

- **Aesthetics:** Good and organized ambiance aids focus, while a bad one makes us anxious.

- **Sensory:** Type of lighting, temperature, sound, smell, color decide the comfort level, relaxed state, or anxiety.

- **People:** Progressive and like-minded people sharing similar objective aid focus. Chatty co-workers and non-aligned people in the surroundings cause distraction.

- **Culture & values**: Conflicting behaviors and non-aligned culture creates a toxic environment. In addition, negative emotions like stress, anxiety, and worry limit the ability to focus.

- **Familiarity**: The absence of known surroundings leads to a lack of clarity. Uncertainty breeds anxiousness, worry, stress and reduces concentration.

Understanding Distraction: A thing that prevents from giving full attention to something else. Hunger, exhaustion, illness, stress, etc., are internal distractions. Social interactions, music, text messages, phone calls, etc., are all external distractions.

The top 12 External distractions at the workplace are as under:

1.Office colleagues: Regular interruptions adversely impact the concentration disrupt the flow of work.

2.Noisy work environment: High noise levels cause distraction from the task at hand.

3.Emails: Receiving email notifications and checking them simultaneously while working on an important project distracts and delays the pace of work.
4.Mobile Phone: Frequently checking the mobile phone during the day diverts attention, interrupts workflow, and causes brain fatigue.

5.Social media: A glaring example of technology ruling brains. Likes, comments, and views aid the dopamine rush leading to high adrenaline. Conversely, lack of engagement causes low self-esteem, stress, worry. Either way, it causes a lack of concentration.

6.Meetings: Excess of meetings breaks the rhythm, reduces concentration.

7.Multi-tasking: It causes strain, making it difficult to concentrate and focus.

8.Messy workplace: Mess at work diverts attention from the creation to surroundings. This acts as a persistent reminder of all that needs to be done.

9.Excessive supervision: Micromanaging things is a dual-edged sword. You lose your precious time interfering in someone else's work. On the other hand, too much control makes the other person conscious and distracts from performing the task efficiently.

10.Comfort: Too much or too little comfort reduces the brain's alertness. Relaxing position reduces brain alertness by inducing sleep. An extremely uncomfortable posture may cause pain and stray the attention from work.

11.Lighting: Dim Lights cause strain on the eyes, reducing concentration. High lights may cause headaches.

12.Temperature: Warm temperature induces sleep, and cold temperature causes uneasiness. Extreme weather conditions are known to make focusing an arduous task.

Assignment 4

---

1. List down the psychological factors limiting your focus and concentration ability.

2. List down the physiological reasons which are stopping you from focusing.

3.List down the external state factors, which interfere with your ability to focus at the workplace or home.

Chapter 4

How to Master the Focus?

"Focus on outcome doesn't get you there; focus on actions does"

-Lalit Hundalani

Clyde Beatty, a lion tamer from over a century ago, learned a lesson that has implications in practically every aspect of our life today.

What was the point of that lesson?

Let's find out what a lion tamer can teach about focusing, concentrating, and living healthier lives.
Clyde Beatty was born in 1903 in Bainbridge, Ohio. He left home as a teenager to join the circus, where he worked as a cage cleaner. Beatty quickly rose from a lowly cage boy to a popular entertainer in the years that followed.

Beatty became well-known for his "fighting act," in which he tamed ferocious wild animals. Beatty's act included a segment where he herded lions, tigers, cougars, and hyenas into the circus ring simultaneously and tamed them all.

Beatty lived into his 60s during a time when the majority of lion tamers died in the ring. In the end, it was cancer, not a lion, that took his life.

How did he make it through? It's all thanks to a simple concept.

One of the first lion tamers to bring a chair into the circus ring was Clyde Beatty.

A lion tamer is typically depicted as an entertainer with a whip and a chair. The whip is the center of attention, but it is mostly for show. In reality, the chair is the one that does the majority of the work.

When a lion tamer places a chair in front of the lion's face, the lion tries to concentrate on all four legs simultaneously. The lion becomes confused and unsure of what to do next because its focus is divided. Instead of attacking the man holding the chair, the lion chooses to freeze and wait when faced with many options.

How many times have you been in the same situation as the lion?

How frequently do you have a goal in mind (for example, losing weight, increasing muscle, starting a business, or travel more), only to become baffled by all of the choices before you and never make any progress?

This is especially true in health, fitness, and medicine, where everyone and everything appears to believe it is their responsibility to complicate matters. Every training regimen you come across is the most effective. Every diet guru claims that their strategy is the best.

As a result, we feel unable to focus or choose the wrong things. We take fewer actions, make less progress, and remain unchanged when we could be developing.

Focus is essentially a muscle. So, if you're wondering how to focus better, it's a skill that must be practiced regularly. That means you'll have to work hard to avoid checking your phone every two minutes if you want to finish that project.

Consider the concept of focus in terms of running. You can't just decide to run a marathon one day; you have to work towards it and train for it.

According to famous Hindu monk, Dandapani we get better at what we practice, and most of us have mastered the art of distraction. Unfortunately, we live in a society that teaches us to multitask and bounce from one task to another without thinking about it. Learning and practicing the art of concentration is an excellent remedy for a world plagued by distraction.

Most people can't concentrate for two reasons:
1.We are never taught how to concentrate.
2.We don't practice concentration.

We are asked to concentrate on studies, food, and everything during our growing up years, but we are never formally taught how to do it. You can't expect someone to know something unless you teach them.

Once you know it, you need to practice it.

We don't practice concentration, we practice distraction 16 hrs a day, seven days a week, and that's why we become pretty good at it. That's the law of practice.

We are never taught concentration, and we never practice it.

We usually blame technology for distraction, while it's a half-truth but not the complete one. Technology is a great enabler, but the problem begins if you surrender yourself to the technology and respond to every notification. Letting technology master your life is the problem and not the technology.

It's a real irony that we have manuals for the smallest of the manufactured gadgets, but there is no manual for the human mind, which is the most complex tool in the world.

To become a focus expert, it's essential to understand the mind. Once we know it, we can control it. Once we can manage it, we can master the focus.

There are two critical things to learn concentration:

- Awareness
- Mind

Consider awareness as the glowing ball of light and mind as the vast field with various chambers. Each chamber is occupied by emotions like anger, jealousy, hunger, greed, sex, joy, happiness, etc. The glowing ball of self-awareness can travel to any area of mind and illuminate it. Whichever room it lights up, we become conscious of it, and the awareness goes up.

When we watch a movie, the story's progression directs our awareness to different areas of our mind. The filmmaker smartly captures our attention and controls the flow of awareness. While in that state, we experience various emotions. Shifting the awareness consistently causes distraction. We go through a similar experience in our daily lives where various factors control our attention, and awareness keeps moving.

Concentration requires keeping the awareness of one particular area for an extended period.
People usually say that my mind wanders, due to which I am unable to focus, which is not correct. Actually, it's the awareness that wanders inside the brain, leading to distraction and not allowing it to concentrate.

Let's do a simple exercise & see how it happens.

Step 1: Close your eyes and become aware of your breath, the chair you are sitting on, the sound of AC, the sound of the fan, and other elements in your surroundings.

Step 2: Think about the latest wedding you attended and the minute details like food, setup, the dress of the bride and groom, and other stuff.

Step 3: Think about your last vacation. The food you ate, the hotel you stayed at, the place you visited, the weather, the experience of the journey, and other things you liked about it.

Step 4: Now, come back to the room and become aware of your surroundings.

Any guesses, what did I just do?

In 4 simple steps, I took control of your awareness and consistently shifted it from one event to another, letting you distract and not allowing you to focus.

This is what happens to us in our day-to-day life, without us realizing it.
Concentration requires letting awareness remain on one particular thing for an extended period.

How to practice concentration?

One of the best ways is to allow awareness to remain on one thing throughout the day. So keep looking for such opportunities throughout the day. For example, while talking to your spouse, partner, friend, or family member, imagine keeping the ball of awareness on them and giving them undivided attention. That's the best way to practice concentration before teaching children to concentrate; we must learn it ourselves. It's necessary to follow the principle of learn, do and teach. Children observe and copy whatever we do. If we don't teach children how to concentrate, they won't know it, and unless they see it, we can't expect them to learn it.

Our life is a manifestation of our energy flow. So make it a point to focus on one thing at a time to manifest what you want in life.

According to Christina Bengtsson, Swedish world champion in precision shooting, focus helps us get the best out of us.

The ability to Focus is usually overlooked, and the human mind struggles to focus on three distinctive counts:

1. Our minds are full of disturbing & negative thoughts. Consciously worried about not being good enough.
2. Instead of focusing on what we are and what we already know, we divert our attention to what we want to achieve and who we want to become.
3. We are frustrated for not having time.

Our mind can traverse in past and future. What if, usually gets us worried and distracts us.

Some of the examples of disturbing thoughts include:

- What if I lose my followers on social media?
- What if I missed the target?
- What if I forgot what to say on stage during the presentation?
- What will people say?

To focus on the present, it's imperative to get rid of these worries about the future and calm yourself.

Focus is choosing the right thought among thousands of ideas going in our minds. To do so, a few simple steps may help:

1.Learn to distinguish between and disturbing and non-disturbing thoughts. One non-disturbing thought can knock off all the disturbing thoughts and bring you back to focus.

2.Constantly being worried about the goal or what we want to achieve shifts focus to the future and drifts us away from the present. Unless we work on what we are good at and remain focused on the present, it's impossible to achieve the future goal. So we end up being trapped in this never-ending loop. Removing the plan for a moment allows us to focus on who we are and what we have(Present) instead of who we want to be and what we want to achieve(Future). It may sound scary at first, as it may seem like a directionless journey. So the focus is about doing what we already know and going about it.

3.We live in an intense time, where we are offered countless possibilities, must do, and must-haves. The fragments of these possibilities provide a plethora of distractions. The thumb rule is more the number of opportunities, the greater the restraint. It’s no longer about prioritizing; instead, it's about non-prioritizing. Replace To do list with Not-To-Do List. We live long term but expect the results in a short time. We put up a post or picture on social media and start chasing for feedback. There is a constant need for external validation without having self-confidence.
To find long term focus for a fulfilled life, we need to start looking inwards. We must become content with our individuality and who we are. As the world gets more intense, in the future, we will have two groups of people :

1.Who co-exist and can handle the intense society.
2.Who become slaves under the same possibilities.

Focus is a vital force that brings out the best in self and others. It is crucial to preserve this skill for future generations.

Mastering the focus requires control of self and managing the external environment. The way to master the focus starts from the mind, travels through the body, and moves out into the outer world.

The following section, which covers the important subject of how to master the focus, is divided into three sections:

- How to train the mind?
- How to train the body?
- How to manage the environment?

How to Train the Mind to Focus?

We have discussed at length in previous sections the critical role played by our mind in influencing the intensity of our focus. Unfortunately, unless controlled, the mind can be distracted easily. This section will evaluate essential methods & techniques that can be used to train the mind to focus better.

1.Mindfulness
2.Meditation
3.Sleep
4.Exercising the brain

1.Mindfulness

Definition of Mindfulness: The ability to be fully present, aware of where we are and what we're doing, and not unduly reactive or overwhelmed by what's happening around us is known as mindfulness. A potent cure to mind wandering and

stress is the tranquil and non-judgmental observation of what is happening around you in the present moment.
It's a simple word to understand. It implies that our mind in its entirety focuses on what's going on, what we're doing, and the environment we're in. Simply put, it prevents the mind from wandering.

Every human being is born with mindfulness; you simply need to learn how to access it. Mindfulness allows the mind to focus on the present with complete awareness. It lets the mind to stabilize in the present scenario, despite high stress. Practicing mindfulness is similar to physical exercise. The more you practice, the greater the results. It teaches the essential skill of paying attention to our attention.

Mindfulness practices use the brain's social wiring to help you tune in to the present moment and create inner peace. As a test, try closing your eyes for three to five minutes and focus on each thought that comes to mind without attempting to modify anything. Simply pay attention to each thought. As you observe your thoughts, you understand they aren't yours, and you aren't deliberately creating them. They're just there, and they don't make you who you are. You'll notice an automatic shift in your capacity to focus if you simply observe them with interest rather than forcing, resisting, or avoiding them. Your muscles may be looser, your heartbeat is slower, and your breathing is gentler.

Key Benefits Of Mindfulness

Mindfulness practice has been linked to a slew of advantages, and the topic's prominence in positive psychology suggests that we'll be seeing a lot more of it in the future.

✓ **Memory Enhancement:** Mindfulness meditation has been empirically related to increased working memory capacity. For example, according to a 2010 study, mindfulness meditation training helped 'buffer' against decreases in working memory capacity when comparing samples of military volunteers who engaged in mindfulness meditation training for eight weeks with those who did not. They also discovered that as the first group practiced mindfulness meditation, their working memory capacity improved. These individuals also reported higher levels of positive affect and lower levels of negative affect.

- ✓ **Meta-cognitive Awareness:** This means being able to step back and recognize one's own sensations and mental processes as ephemeral, instantaneous happenings rather than "who we are." This would be related to 'knowing' and 'freeing' the mind in a Buddhist sense.

- ✓ **Reduced Anxiety:** Mindfulness practice has been known to lessen anxiety and depression levels. Thereby improving self-esteem.

- ✓ **Low Emotional Reactivity:** There's also evidence that mindfulness meditation can help with emotional 'reactivity.' Ortner and colleagues conducted a dynamic interference experiment in 2007 in which participants with varying levels of mindfulness meditation experience were asked to evaluate tones that were supplied 1 or 4 seconds after a neutral or emotionally disturbing visual was presented. Those who had more experience with mindfulness meditation were better able to emotionally detach, meaning they were more focused on the job at hand even when emotionally painful images were shown.

- ✓ **Visual Attention Processing:** Hodgins and Adair (2010) conducted another study to compare the performance of 'meditators' and 'non-meditators on visual attention processing tasks. Again, mindfulness meditation practitioners demonstrated improved attentional functioning on assessments of concentration, selective attention, and other areas. These findings support previous research that shows systematic mindfulness meditation training improves attention, awareness, and emotion.

- ✓ **Stress Reduction:** Stress reduction has also been connected to mindfulness training. For example, it has been observed that cancer patients who participated in mindfulness training had much lower self-reported stress than those who did not. They also showed more positive moods and fewer post-traumatic avoidance indicators, including a lack of interest in activities.

- ✓ **Reduction of Physical Pain:** Mindfulness has also been linked to a decrease in perceived pain. In addition, numerous studies show how mindfulness can help patients manage chronic pain and enhance their quality of life. Indeed, there are several pieces of research on issues such as reduced psychological distress and increased focus and numerous applications of the above concepts in a variety of settings.

There are lots of scientific data in your favor whether you want to practice mindfulness to deal with anxiety or stress or if you want to improve your attentional skills. Mindfulness can aid in treating depression, enhancing psychological well-being, managing physical pain, and even memory improvement. When it comes to our thoughts and feelings, being aware of our emotions allows us to shift to more positive mindsets and work toward becoming a better—or at the very least, happier—person.

In at least two ways, mindfulness can help us enhance our mental health. First, mindfulness-based therapy and interventions take a more systematic approach to treating mental health problems. Let's take a quick look at both.

Given that anxiety and depression are two of the most common mental diseases worldwide, it's no surprise that two of the most well-known mindfulness-based treatment target these mental states.

Mindfulness-Based Stress Reduction (MBSR) is a group technique. It is based on the premise that a diverse set of mindfulness practices can be used to assist people in coping with the challenges of stress and anxiety-related mental disease. Typically, this will include a mixture of yoga, mindfulness meditation, and other stress-relieving activities.

Mindfulness-Based Cognitive Therapy (MBCT) is a group therapy that helps people with recurrent depression reduce symptoms and avoid relapse. Cognitive-behavioral therapy (CBT) and mindfulness activities, such as mindful breathing and meditation, are used in MBCT. In addition, acceptance is a crucial component of MBCT since participants learn techniques for re-framing their feelings rather than eradicating them.

Common Mindfulness Techniques

- ***Focused attention on your breath*** is a type of mindfulness that cultivates present-mindedness that extends to our work routine and interpersonal relationships. Close your eyes and take a few deep breaths in and out, concentrating on each inhale and exhale. Follow your breath from the beginning of an inhalation, when your lungs are full, to the end, when they are empty. Then begin the process all over again. Thoughts typically occur after five minutes of doing this cycle. After that, you can question if you're doing the exercise correctly, be concerned about an incomplete project, or wonder if it's worth your time given everything else on your plate.

Accept anything that comes your way with an open heart. Simply step out of the thought stream and softly return to the sensations of your breath whenever your mind wanders and becomes trapped in a chain of thoughts (this is a natural aspect of the meditation process). Slowly open your eyes after five minutes and take in the colors and textures around you. Then extend and breathe into your vivid awareness, noticing how much more connected to the moment you feel, as well as how peaceful, clear-headed, and re-energized you are.

Open awareness is another mindfulness approach for staying focused in the present moment without taking time away from your job routines. Just 60 seconds of open awareness mindfulness can help you relax, cleanse your mind, and boost vitality. Pay attention to the many sounds around you, as well as flowers, trees, or other aspects of nature. Take note of the exact position at your workstation where the floor or the back of your chair supports your back. Focus on the sensations of your feet within your shoes and the carpet beneath your feet as you walk.

Illustrations for practicing Mindfulness in daily lives

a)Walking: Using the mindfulness guidelines as a guide, there are various ways that awareness and non-judgmental contemplation may turn even the most routine routines into enjoyable experiences. For example, take careful note of each step as you walk to work or the store. Draw your awareness to what you're doing rather than allowing your mind to wander into thought patterns or processes. Take note of how each step feels, how the breeze ruffles your clothes or brushes your skin. Listen to the noises and see the colors as you go past trees or water. All of these should be experienced with attention in the present moment.

b)Interactions: Let's take the example of Kim and Kong to demonstrate how non-judgmental tuning shows mindfulness at work. Kim is dissatisfied with Kong and attempts to explain himself. Kong can listen without criticizing him, even if his comments are a little jumbled and full of emotion. Rather than arguing without listening, this allows them to arrive at a more constructive conclusion while expanding their relationship and increasing trust.

c)Before a public appearance: Many of us are intimidated by public speaking, and that's fine. Start with some slow breathing if you want to practice mindfulness to help you deal with the stress you're experiencing. Then, find a quiet place where you may take a moment to reflect on how you're feeling. Rather than focusing on negative ideas, attempt to decentre—accept and admit that this is how you're feeling but not who you are.
You might want to direct your attention to the physical feelings you're having, focusing on each region of your body as you relax it. Please take note of how it feels when your muscles relax, and your stress dissipates.

Tips for Practicing Mindfulness

1. **Mindful Breathing**: Spend a few moments focusing on your breathing. Observe how your breath goes in and out, as well as how your tummy rises and falls with each breath.

2. **Engagement in the Task**: Make a mental note of anything you're doing. What are your senses, not your thoughts, telling you while you're sitting, eating, or relaxing? Take note of the present moment. If you're stretching, for example, take note of how each movement makes your body feel. When you're eating, concentrate on the flavor, color, and texture of your food.

3.Savour the process: Focus on the present moment if you're heading somewhere. Instead of allowing your mind to wander, please bring it back to the actual act of walking. What are your thoughts? Pay greater attention to what you're doing as you step and how your feet feel, rather than where you're going. On sand or grass, this is a fun one to attempt.

4. **Do nothing**: You don't have to be doing something all of the time. Simply exist and unwind. This is, after all, about the here and now.

5. **Rewind:** If you find yourself thinking again, simply return your attention to your breathing. Return your attention to how your breath enters and exits your body, and if you can relax your muscles while doing so, nothing like it.
6. **Mindful of the cognitive process**: Recognize that your mental processes are just that: thoughts. They aren't always accurate, and they don't need you to act. Mindfulness is about simply being present in the moment and accepting things as they are. Internally, this is also true—all it's part of knowing your mind.

7. **Self-consciousness:** You might realize that you're becoming more conscious of your own emotions and thoughts. Accept them without judging them.

8.Heightened awareness: You may discover that certain activities cause you to lose interest. These are excellent opportunities to increase your understanding. This is an example of how mindfulness practice may be incorporated into your daily routine in various ways. For example, mindfulness can be practiced while driving, walking, swimming, or even brushing your teeth.

9.Immersion in nature: Relaxing circumstances can make it easier to tune in. Plus, being in nature has a plethora of health benefits!

10. Observe the drift: Allow yourself to observe when your mind returns to judgment. Remember that this is entirely normal and does not have to be a part of your identity. Freeing your mind from practices like judgment is a part of mindfulness practice. With time and practice, you may find that this becomes simpler.

Apart from mindfulness, another important technique for training the mind to improve concentration and focus is meditation. Let's evaluate the efficacy of this process to our object.

2.Meditation

Meditation is a series of techniques designed to promote heightened awareness and focused concentration. Meditation is another strategy for altering understanding that has been found to provide a variety of psychological advantages.

Meditation has been practiced for thousands of years in cultures all around the world. Likewise, it has a long history in nearly every religion, including Buddhism, Hinduism, Christianity, Judaism, and Islam. Although meditation is frequently utilized for religious purposes, many people employ it regardless of their religious or spiritual views or practices. Meditation can also be used as a form of psychotherapy.

Meditation concepts

1.Choose a peaceful, distraction-free location. Disconnect from your phone, television, and other sources of distraction. If you want to listen to music quietly, consider something soothing and repetitious.
2. If you're beginning to start, you might want to limit yourself to shorter sessions of 5 to 10 minutes.

3. Pay attention to your body and make yourself at ease. You can sit cross-legged on the floor or in a chair for as long as you feel comfortable posing for several minutes.

4.Keep your attention on your breathing. Exhale slowly after taking deep breaths that stretch your belly. Pay attention to the sensations of each breath.

5.Take note of your thoughts. The goal of meditation is not to clear your mind because your mind will eventually wander. Instead, whenever you sense your mind drifting, softly bring your attention back to your breath. Don't criticize or analyze your ideas; instead, return your attention to your deep breathing.

Meditation comes in a variety of forms. Although there are many various styles of meditation, there are two primary varieties:

1.Concentrative meditation
2.Mindfulness meditation

1.Concentrative meditation entails focusing your full attention on a single item while tuning out everything else. To achieve a higher state of being, the goal is to truly experience whatever you're focusing on, whether it's your breath, a single word, or a mantra.

Basic steps involved in concentrative meditation:

- **Choose the target:** Focusing on your breath is usually the first step in any meditation practice; it's a fantastic choice.
- **Choose a position**: Sit in a straight position. For example, sit on the edge of a chair, relaxing into your pelvic bones with your feet on the floor. If you're

sitting on the ground, use a pillow or block to raise yourself so your thighs are relaxed and your spine remains tall.

- **Get into a relaxed state**: Relax your shoulders and breathe deeply from your belly button. You can cross your legs if you like, but you don't have to if another posture is more comfortable for you, as long as you can fully relax without falling asleep.
- **Pay attention to the target:** Focus on the senses of your focused point, such as sound, smell, sight, and details. The objective is to experience it simply and be fully present at the moment rather than think about it. For example, pay attention to the sensations you have as you inhale and exhale each breath if you're concentrating on your breath.
- **Stop the self-talk**: If your internal monologue begins to analyze your target or review stressful incidents from the day, worry about the future, write a grocery list, or anything else, gently return your focus to your chosen target and the experience it offers. You may be concentrating on something, but the idea is to keep your thoughts silent.
- **Eliminate the fear of failure**: Don't allow your inner perfectionist to beat you up for doing it "wrong" if you discover your mind engaging you and realize you're not entirely present with the sensations of your chosen focus. Instead, simply praise yourself for observing and redirect your attention to the present moment and your feelings.

2.Mindfulness Meditation: Mindfulness meditation is a mental training technique that helps relax your mind and body by slowing down racing thoughts, letting go of negativity, and focusing on the present moment. It blends meditation with mindfulness. It is defined as a mental state in which you are entirely focused on "the present" and can accept and acknowledge your thoughts, feelings, and sensations without judgment.

Mindfulness meditation involves deep breathing and awareness of the body and mind. Techniques vary, but in general, it involves deep breathing and understanding of the body and mind. Mindfulness meditation does not necessitate any props or preparation (no need for candles, essential oils, or mantras, unless you enjoy them).

Mindfulness-based stress reduction (MBSR) and mindfulness-based cognitive therapy (MBCT) are examples of mindfulness meditation. It can be used to address various disorders, such as depression; the focus of each practice may vary. Overall, it entails being aware of and active in the current moment and being open, conscious, and accepting of yourself.

Although you can learn mindfulness meditation on your own, a teacher or program can also assist you in getting started, especially if you're practicing meditation for health reasons. Here are some basic instructions to get you started on your own:

a. **Choose a comfortable position**: Locate a quiet and pleasant location. Sit with your head, neck, and back upright but not stiff in a chair or on the floor. It's also a good idea to dress comfortably and loosely so you don't become side-tracked. However, because this exercise may be done anywhere, any time, there is no need to dress up.

b. **Set a timer or alarm clock:** While a timer isn't mandatory, it can help you focus on meditation and forget about time, as well as eliminate any excuses you might have for stopping and doing something else. It can help ensure you're not meditating for too long because many people lose the sense of time while meditating. Allow yourself time after meditation to become aware of your surroundings and gradually rise. While some people meditate for more extended periods, even a few minutes a day can help. Begin with a 5-minute meditation session and gradually expand the duration of your sessions by 10 or 15 minutes until you can meditate for 30 minutes at a time.

c. **Notice your breathing:** Tune to the feel of air moving in and out of your body while you breathe by becoming aware of your breath. As the air enters and leaves your nostrils, feel your belly rise and fall. Pay attention to the temperature difference between inhaled and expelled breaths.

d. **Notice your thoughts:** The idea is to become more comfortable with being a "witness" to your ideas rather than trying to stop them. Don't ignore or suppress thoughts that arise in your head. Simply take notice of them, be calm, and use your breathing as a stabilizing force. Consider your ideas to be clouds going by; see how they shift and alter as they float by. While you're meditating, repeat this as many times as you need to.

e. **Take a break:** If you find yourself being carried away in your thoughts—whether with worry, fear, anxiety, or hope—return to your breathing and examine where your mind went without passing judgment. Don't be too hard on yourself if this happens; mindfulness is the habit of returning to your breath and refocusing on the present moment.

Tips for practicing mindfulness meditation

Finding methods to incorporate mindfulness into your daily life becomes easier as you practice mindfulness meditation—especially on those days when life is too busy to carve out a minute alone. One way is mindfulness meditation, although there are many possibilities for mindfulness in everyday activities and duties, such as:

A. **Brushing your Teeth**: Feel your feet on the floor, the brush in your hand, and your arm moving up and down while you brush your teeth.
B. **Dishwashing**: Enjoy the sensation of warm water on your hands, the sight of bubbles, and the sound of pans clattering on the sink's bottom.
C. **Washing Clothes**: When doing laundry, pay attention to how the clean clothing smells and the fabric feels. As you fold laundry, add a focused aspect by counting your breaths.
D. **Driving**: Turn off the radio or listen to relaxing, such as classical music while driving. Find the halfway point between relaxing your hands and clutching the wheel too tightly by imagining your spine rising taller. Bring your attention back to where you and your automobile are in space whenever you notice your mind drifting.
E. **Working Out**: Instead of watching television while exercising on the treadmill, concentrate on your breathing and where your feet are as you go.
F. **Putting kids to sleep**: Preparing the youngsters for bed: Get down on your children's level, look them in the eyes, listen more than you speak, and appreciate any snuggles. They will relax if you relax.

How Meditation improves Focus?

Researchers utilized various tests to see how frequent meditation impacts people's capacity to control their attention. People who started meditating a few months back scored better on tasks requiring cutting off distractions. Long-term meditators showed a dramatically increased ability to retain focus for unusually long periods.

Meditation can help improve brain structure. It rewires our neural circuits. It prunes away the least used connections and strengthening the ones, which are used more often. Experiments suggest that Buddhist monks have powerful connections between scattered regions in their brains, which allows for more synchronized communication. Expert meditators also seem to develop a wrinkly cortex, which is the brain's outer layer. The cortex is utilized in many of the brain's mental abilities. Several studies have confirmed that meditation can increase the volume and density of the hippocampus, a seahorse-shaped area in the middle of the skull inside our brain, which is crucial for memory. Meditation counteracts the decay of regions responsible for memory and retention of information.

Several studies have proved that meditation for as little as 12-20 minutes per day consistently can sharpen the mind. In addition, in some tests of visual attention, it was confirmed that expert meditators in their 50's & 60's could outperform the non-meditators in their 20's & 30's.

Changes in the brain structure

Neuroscientists began utilizing fMRI machines and other brain scanners to examine inside the minds of people who had been practicing mindfulness meditation for years about a decade ago to discover more about the brain mechanisms driving these improvements. When they did, they found that their brains differed significantly from those of non-meditators.

Since then, more than 20 similar investigations have been undertaken. Some of their findings have been contradictory, but a recent meta-analysis conducted by Kieran Fox of the University of British Columbia discovered that experienced meditators have unique variations in eight brain areas compared to non-meditators.

The most noticeable difference is an increase in tissue in the anterior cingulate cortex, known to sustain attention and impulse control. Other research has discovered that meditators had denser tissue in cortex areas linked to attention regulation and body awareness. In addition, regular meditation has been linked to reducing the size of the right amygdala, a brain area involved in processing negative emotions, including fear.

According to some research, meditators have lower activity in the insula — a brain region involved for pain perception — than non-meditators, which could explain why they report feeling less pain when subjected to the same painful stimuli (such as placing their hands in a pail of ice-cold water).

With this, we conclude the discussion on the second important technique for conditioning the brain to concentrate and focus better. The third most crucial aspect vital for brain health is sleep. So, let's delve deeper to understand better.

3.Sleep

When you sleep, your body goes through a sequence of changes that allow you to get the rest you need. Sleep permits the brain and body to settle down and engage in healing processes, resulting in improved physical and mental performance the next day and over time. When you don't get enough sleep, these essential functions are disrupted, affecting your thinking, concentration, energy levels, and mood. As a result, getting the proper amount of sleep is critical – seven to nine hours for adults and even more for children and teenagers. Sleep's intricacy and relevance for our well-being are demonstrated by what happens during sleep, including how different stages of sleep develop.

You go through four to five sleep cycles in a typical night's sleep. There are four distinct sleep stages in each sleep cycle.

The four stages of sleep are further divided into two categories: REM (rapid eye movement) and non-REM (non-rapid eye movement) sleep. These distinctions are critical because what occurs during REM sleep differs significantly from what happens during non-REM periods.

Non-REM activity dominates the first three stages of sleep. The first stage is brief, and it depicts the act of dozing asleep and transitioning into sleep. As you fall asleep in Stage 2, your body and mind begin to calm down. During the first two levels, it's simplest to be awakened.

REM sleep is the fourth stage of sleep. Brain activity spikes back up to levels similar to when you're awake during REM periods, explaining why REM is linked to the most vivid dreams. While our heart rate and breathing rate increase during REM sleep, most of our muscles remain paralyzed, preventing us from acting out our fantasies.

Each sleep cycle might last anywhere from 70 to 120 minutes. Non-REM sleep takes up more time in the early sleep cycles of the night. The second half of the night is when the majority of REM sleep occurs.

During sleep, virtually every component of the body undergoes significant changes. For example, thousands of neurons in the brain transform from waking to sleeping mode when you fall asleep, sending impulses all through your body.

While the biological purpose of sleep is yet unknown, research shows that it strengthens the cardiovascular and immunological systems and aids in metabolism regulation. Changes in key biological systems can be seen as a result of what happens during sleep.

Brain waves indicate distinct patterns linked with each sleep stage when measured during sleep. For example, brain waves slow down significantly in the early stages of non-REM sleep; yet, there are frequent short bursts of brain activity in Stages 2 and 3.

During REM sleep, brain activity speeds up, resulting in distinct types of brain waves. Because of the increased brain activity, REM sleep is known as the state most closely related to vivid dreams. Even with reduced brain activity, non-REM sleep is assumed to support healthy brain function while awake. In contrast, REM sleep is expected to support critical cognitive abilities, including memory consolidation.

According to the brain plasticity theory, sleep is necessary for brain function. It permits your neurons, or nerve cells, to restructure specifically. The glymphatic (waste clearing) system in your brain clears waste from the central nervous system as you sleep. It clears your brain of harmful byproducts that accumulate throughout the day. This enables your brain to function properly when you wake up.

According to research, sleep aids memory function by transforming short-term memories into long-term memories and eliminating (or forgetting) unnecessary information that would otherwise clog the nervous system.

The key benefits of sleep are summarized as under:

- ✓ **Improved brain efficiency:** Getting enough quality sleep helps your brain fire on all cylinders when you're awake, allowing you to think and respond faster and with fewer errors. This may be because sleep enables the neurons you've been utilizing all day to rest and repair themselves before you rely on them again the next day. Because everything, including the tiniest neurons, requires rest at some point. However, once they've had a chance to relax, you'll find it simpler to concentrate and remember things. According to a study published in the National Library of Medicine, you'll also be less inclined to give up when it comes to tackling a difficult task.

Researchers at the City University of New York presented college students with a series of math tasks after a night of good sleep and then again after a night of insufficient sleep. In the second scenario, the students didn't perform well and preferred to choose less complicated exercises after not obtaining enough sleep.

In other words, they were aware that they weren't as bright as they considered themselves to be. So, they tried to avoid failing by adopting a less challenging path. That's OK for an experiment, but it's hardly the kind of behavior that'll get you a promotion at work.

✓ **The clarity to comprehend information:** Whether you believe it or not, your brain can understand detailed information while you sleep. Experts have long known that even when your brain is engaged in the sleep process, it maintains some level of consciousness. Sleeping persons, for example, are more likely to respond to their names or startling sounds such as a fire alarm or an alarm clock than to other noises. But, according to a ground-breaking study published recently in the journal Current Biology, that's just the start. Researchers instructed study participants to categorize uttered words by pushing a left or right button while lying in a dark room. Then, after the individuals had nodded asleep, the researchers presented them with new words that fit into the same categories as the words they had heard while awake. What's the strangest thing? Even as the participants were sleeping, brain monitoring devices revealed that their brains were processing the information they had learned to identify left or right words.

The individuals had no recollection of hearing the new words while sleeping when they were awake. In other words, while the subjects were entirely unaware, their brains absorbed all of the latest information. That is to say, your brain continues to learn even while you sleep.

- ✓ **Memory retention:** Imagine having to stop what you were doing every time you did or experienced something new throughout the day to file it away in your short- or long-term memory file so you could retrieve it later when you needed it. You'd probably spend so much time documenting your life that you'd never get anything else done. You don't have to do that because of the power of sleep. This is because snooze time is when your brain is most active, processing memories. Your brain attempts to cement memories created throughout the day as you sleep.

  When you sleep, your brain selects what events from the day are worth remembering—and what events from the day are worth forgetting so you can make room for new information the next day. When you think about it, it makes perfect sense. But it's more than a hypothesis. According to German researchers in a 2013 analysis, more than a century of research reveals that sleep increases memory retention—so much so that the brain can be more efficient at consolidating memories when you're asleep than when you're awake.

Regrettably, the opposite is also true. As you get older, your sleep patterns change, and so does your ability to develop new memories. As a result, memory-cementing skills can start to deteriorate as early as your late thirties, and it only gets worse from there. For example, people over the age of 60 experienced a 70 percent loss in a deep sleep compared to adults ages 18 to 25, according to a study published in the journal Nature Neuroscience, and thus had a more challenging time recalling things the next day.

Even so, just because you're getting older doesn't mean you'll live a life of utter forgetfulness. While some memory loss is unavoidable with age, obtaining adequate sleep is critical for making the most of your brain's memory-consolidating abilities. On most nights, try to get seven to eight hours of sleep, especially on days when you've learned something new.

✓ **Alleviates creativity:** On days when you don't get enough sleep, your thoughts are likely to go something like this: "I'm so exhausted." This is something I can't do right now. "All I want to do now is go home and do nothing."
When you're focused on climbing into bed and getting some much-needed rest, coming up with fascinating new ideas is usually the last thing on your mind. Unfortunately, sleep deprivation impairs your ability to be creative because it reduces your ability to think creatively. There's a lot more to it than that, of course.

While you sleep, your brain is busy consolidating memories and establishing connections between new and old concepts, preparing you for that all-important light bulb moment. This is supported by a study published in the National Academy of Sciences of the United States of America. Study participants were 33 percent more successful at completing tasks that required them to create uncommonly (read: creative) connections in their brain after a night of restful sleep than those who hadn't. Stage 5 (or REM sleep)—the period of the sleep cycle that involves dreaming—is, predictably, essential for increasing creativity.

According to a recent study presented at the American Psychological Association, people who took 90-minute naps that included REM sleep performed 40 percent better on word problems that required them to see connections between seemingly unrelated words than people who didn't nap at all annual conventions. According to academics, this could be because REM sleep allows your brain to "detach" your recollection of a word's meaning and apply it to a new context.

- ✓ **Flushing out toxins from the brain:** The term "toxin" is frequently used these days. And in health-related circles, there are many remedies promoted as beneficial for eliminating toxins from the body. (We're talking about juice fasts, activated charcoal, and apple cider vinegar). For the time being, it's debatable if any of those measures are genuinely successful. But when it comes to getting rid of toxins, one thing that has been proven to work is getting enough sleep. At the same time that your brain is busy sending out growth hormones, consolidating memories, and building creativity-boosting connections, it's also cleaning up any undesirable filth.

According to Dr. John Medina, a developmental molecular biologist and author of the New York Times bestseller Brain Rules: 12 Principles for Surviving and Thriving at Work, Home, and School, "there is evidence the brain clears out toxic wastes accumulated during the day at night, through the convective motion of the fluid that bathes the brain." "You won't have the molecular waste cleared if you don't sleep," he adds.

How to get the sleep that your brain needs?

Consider yourself at work, attempting to complete a critical project. You're clacking away on your keyboard, wholly immersed in your work–until a coworker enters your cubicle and stands in front of your computer screen. Then, you suddenly find yourself unable to complete your tasks because someone is literally blocking your way. Similarly, sleep is the process when your brain finishes all of its critical work, allowing you to function like a healthy, productive human during the day rather than a zombie.

However, if you stay up late or do other things that make it difficult to fall asleep (such as drinking a lot of caffeine before bed or spending a lot of time in front of electronic gadgets), you become the coworker in front of the computer screen. Your brain can't get its work done because of your unhealthy habits. So, how much sleep do you require? Everyone is unique in their way. While some people can't function at their best with fewer than nine hours of sleep, others may get by with just seven.

And anything in that range is considered healthy, so it's just a matter of trying different things to see how you react. For example, if you're weary or groggy during the day, you're not getting enough sleep, so try adding some additional time and going to bed to see if you're more aware.

However, if you're having difficulties sleeping, the solution may not be so obvious. For example, if you're already sleeping for eight and a half or nine hours, it might be time to move your bedtime forward a few hours. But, more than likely, you're having difficulties sleeping because you're agitated, or because you're exposed to too much energetic stimulus at night, or because you're simply uncomfortable.

Also, don't forget about what you sleep on. You can follow all of the best sleep health guidelines in the world, but high-quality sleep will be difficult to come by if you sleep on a rock. Finding a supportive, comfy mattress will go a long way toward improving your sleep.

4.Brain Exercises to Strengthen Focus

It has been rightly said that focus is like a muscle. The way working on our body helps us in developing muscles and makes us stronger. Same way, exercising the brain sharpens attention and makes us more focused. Simple everyday exercises come in handy and get the required results.

There are numerous ways to sharpen our mental acuity and keep the brain healthy, regardless of age. Specific brain exercises that improve memory, concentration, and attention can help complete daily chores faster and more efficiently and maintain the mind fresh as we age.

- **Solve Puzzles:** Working on a jigsaw puzzle is a wonderful way to exercise your brain, whether you're putting together an image of the Eiffel Tower or combining pieces to construct a dinosaur. Jigsaw puzzles employ many cognitive capacities and are a protective factor for visuospatial cognitive aging.

  To put it another way, when putting together a jigsaw puzzle, you must examine individual parts and determine where they go into the bigger picture. Again, this might be an excellent method to stretch and challenge your mind.

- **Card Games:** The game of cards is one of the most mentally stimulating activities for humans. It can increase brain capacity in numerous areas and boost memory and cognitive abilities. In addition, traditional games like solitaire, bridge, rummy, poker, hearts, etc., are easy to learn and practice.

- **Building vocabulary:** An extensive vocabulary makes you sound intelligent but is also an effective brain exercise. Many brain regions are involved in vocabulary activities, notably in critical visual and auditory processing areas. Try this brain-boosting activity to put this hypothesis to the test-When you're reading, keep a notebook with you. Please make a list of one unknown word, then check it up in the dictionary. Then, the next day, try to utilize that word five times.

- **Leveraging senses:** Engaging all of our senses assists in developing our brain. Try practicing tasks that involve all five of your senses simultaneously to work your senses and your brain. Activities like baking a cake or cookies, trying a new exotic dish, visiting a vegetable market need utilization of all the senses-smell, touch, taste, seeing, and hear simultaneously.

- **Learn a skill:** Learning a new skill is not only enjoyable and exciting, but it may also aid in enhancing your brain's connections. Learning a new skill can also help improve memory performance in older persons. A new software application, how to swim, horse riding, dancing, writing a book, etc., the range is unlimited. Just pick up something which you always wanted to learn and go with it.

- **Teach a skill:** One of the most effective methods to broaden your knowledge is to teach a skill to someone else. You must practice a new skill after learning it. It demands you to explain the topic and rectify any errors you make when teaching it to someone else. Learn to write a book, for example, and then teach a friend how to do so.

- **Play or listen to music:** Listening to cheerful music generates more imaginative solutions than listening to silence. It can help you think more creatively and enhance your brain function. And if you've always wanted to learn to play music, now is a fantastic moment to start because your brain can learn new skills at any age. That is why it is never too late to learn to play an instrument such as the piano, guitar, or even the drums.

- **Explore variety in the routine:** When it comes to your daily tasks, don't become stuck in a rut. Instead, be open to trying fresh approaches to the same functions. For example, each week, take a different route to work or attempt another transportation method, such as biking or taking public transit instead of driving. This slight shift can improve your brain, and you might be amazed at how simple it is to modify your thinking.

- **Learn a new language:** Researches have overwhelmingly confirmed the significant cognitive benefits of speaking more than one language. According to multiple studies, bilingualism has been linked to superior memory, visual-spatial skills, and higher levels of creativity. Fluency in multiple languages can also help you move between tasks more readily and postpone the start of age-related mental deterioration. According to studies, learning a new language can help you improve your memory and other brain skills at any time in your life.

- **Concentrate on others:** Take notice of four facts about someone the next time you interact with them. Perhaps you notice their shirt or pants color. Do they have spectacles on? Is there a hat on them, and if so, what kind? How about the hair color? Make a mental note of the four things you want to remember and return to it later in the day. Finally, make a list of what you recall about those four details.

No matter your age, focusing on your brain health is one of the most effective ways to increase concentration, focus, memory, and mental agility. In addition, you'll be challenging your mind, sharpening your cognitive skills, and potentially learning something new and enriching along the way if you incorporate brain workouts into your daily life.

How to Train the Body to Focus?

The two main elements which play a vital role in preparing the body and improving concentration are:

1.Exercise
2.Nutrition

1.Exercise

Physical workouts have always been known for boosting energy levels, which is essential for enhanced focus levels. The physical advantages of exercise are self-evident. On the other hand, the mental ones have the potential to transform your capacity to focus and be more productive at work.
It's not simply about aerobic ability and muscle mass when it comes to exercise. Yes, exercise can improve your physical health and physique, help you lose weight, improve your sexual life, and even add years to your life. However, most people are not motivated to stay active by this.

- ✓ **Enhances Energy:** At first, this one appears to be counterintuitive. Isn't exercise supposed to make you tired? No, not at all. Workout encourages the growth of mitochondria, your cells' "powerhouses." Mitochondria, in turn, create the chemical that your body uses as an energy source (ATP). This not only gives the body more energy, but it also gives the brain more energy.

- ✓ **Enhances Your Mood:** Physical activity causes the release of a cocktail of neurotransmitters in the brain. Scientists haven't figured out why this happens yet, but the consequences are apparent. These feel-good molecules can have a significant impact on how you feel. As a result, the mythical "runner's high" exists. The improved mood is a good advantage in and of itself, but it also leads to higher productivity. Not to mention that your interactions with co-workers will likely improve, reducing drama and allowing you to accomplish more as a team.

- ✓ **Defends Against Illnesses:** It's challenging to be productive when you're locked in bed, unable to move due to whatever ailment is circulating at the time. Exercising regularly may assist you in staying in the game. A 12-week study published in the British Journal of Sports Medicine monitored a sample of 1,002 healthy adults and discovered that those who exercised frequently had fewer (and less severe) upper respiratory tract sickness symptoms than those who did not.

- ✓ **Increases memory, cognition, and learning:** Today's knowledge worker has ongoing challenges in keeping up with new processes and technologies. Those who commit to lifelong learning will flourish in this information economy.

  It's one thing to be willing. However, exercise can assist you in making it a reality. According to a study from the University of British Columbia, regular aerobic exercise (the kind that gets your pulse racing) increases the size of the hippocampus, the brain area involved in learning and verbal memory.

  If you make exercise a lifelong habit, you will reap even more benefits. The ability of the body to produce new brain cells (a process known as neurogenesis) decreases with age. However, some intriguing mouse study suggests that exercise may be able to help avoid this deterioration. As a result, once you reach your 50s, 60s, or 70s, you may have more brain cells than your sedentary colleagues.

Regular exercise has been shown to help those with depression, anxiety, and ADHD. It also helps to relax, improves your memory, sleep better, and enhances your general mood. You don't have to be a fitness enthusiast to receive the rewards. According to research, even small quantities of exercise can make a significant difference. You may learn to use exercise as a reliable tool to deal with mental health issues, increase your energy and attitude, and get more out of life, regardless of your age or fitness level.

Some of the mental health conditions where exercise helps are as under:

- ✓ **Depression:** Studies have shown exercise to be as helpful as antidepressant medication in treating mild to moderate depression without adverse effects. For instance, a recent study from the Harvard T.H. Chan School of Public Health discovered that running for 15 minutes or walking for an hour each day reduced the risk of severe depression by 26%. In addition to alleviating depression symptoms, studies show that sticking to an exercise routine can help you avoid relapsing.

  For a variety of reasons, exercise is an effective antidepressant. It also causes your brain to release endorphins, which are potent molecules that excite you and make you feel happy. Finally, exercise can work as a diversion, allowing you to find some quiet time to interrupt the loop of negative thoughts that contribute to sadness.

- ✓ **Anxiety:** Exercise is an anti-anxiety treatment that is both natural and effective. The release of endorphins relieves tension and stress, increases physical and mental vitality, and improves overall well-being. Of course, anything that gets you moving can help, but paying attention rather than zoning out will provide a more significant benefit. For example, try paying attention to the sensation of your feet hitting the ground, the rhythm of your breathing, or the feel of the wind on your skin. You'll not only improve your physical condition faster by adding this mindfulness element—focusing on your body and how it feels when you exercise—but you'll also be able to break the flow of constant anxieties going through your head.

- ✓ **Stress:** Have you ever observed how your body reacts to stress? Your muscles, particularly those in your face, neck, and shoulders, may be stiff, causing back or neck pain, as well as unpleasant headaches. You may experience chest tightness, a hammering pulse, or muscle cramps. Insomnia, heartburn, stomachache, diarrhea, or excessive urination are all possible side effects. These physical symptoms can cause anxiety and discomfort, leading to even more stress, creating a vicious loop between your mind and body. Exercising is an excellent method to get out of this rut. Physical activity helps relax the muscles and release stress in the body and produce endorphins in the brain. Because the body and mind are so intertwined, your mind will know as well when your body feels better.

- ✓ **Attention-Deficit-Hyperactivity-Disorder:** Regular exercise is one of the most simple and effective strategies to alleviate ADHD symptoms and improve concentration, motivation, memory, and mood. Physical activity raises dopamine, norepinephrine, and serotonin levels in the brain, all of which affect focus and attention. Exercise acts similarly to ADHD drugs like Ritalin and Adderall in this regard.

- ✓ **Trauma:** Evidence suggests that focusing on your body and how it feels when exercising can help your nervous system become "unstuck" and begin to move out of the immobility stress response associated with trauma. Instead of allowing your mind to wander, focus on the physical sensations in your joints and muscles, as well as your insides, while you move your body. Cross-movement exercises that work both arms and legs, such as walking (particularly in sand), jogging, swimming, weight training, or dancing, are the best options.

To gain physical and mental health advantages, you don't need to take hours out of your busy day to go to the gym, sweat buckets, or run mile after mile. It's enough to do 30-minutes of moderate activity five times a week. It can also be broken down into two 15-minute or even three 10-minute workout sessions.

Begin with 5- or 10-minute sessions and gradually increase the length of time. You'll have more energy as you work out, so you'll eventually be ready for a little more. The goal is to commit to some modest physical activity on most days, no matter how little. You can gradually increase the amount of time you spend exercising or attempt other types of activities as your habit develops. The benefits of exercise will begin to pay off if you stick with it.

How to start with physical activity?

Even in the best of times, many of us find it challenging to encourage ourselves to exercise. It's even more challenging when you're depressed, anxious, agitated, or dealing with another mental health issue. This is especially true of sadness and anxiety, making you feel imprisoned in a vicious cycle. Of course, you know that exercise would help you feel better. Still, sadness has sapped your energy and enthusiasm to exercise, or your social anxiety prevents you from attending an exercise class or going for a run in the park.

- ✓ **Begin small**. Setting lofty goals like running a marathon or working out for an hour every morning when you're suffering from anxiety or depression and haven't exercised in a long time will only make you feel worse if you fall short. Instead, it's better to start small and work your way up.

- ✓ **Workouts in your high state**. Perhaps you have the most power in the morning before going to work or school or at lunchtime before the mid-afternoon slump sets in? Maybe you're better at exercising for more extended periods on weekends. If you're exhausted and unmotivated all day due to depression or anxiety, try dancing to music or simply going for a stroll. Even a 15-minute walk can help you clear your mind, enhance your mood and increase your vitality. As you move and begin to feel better, you'll likely find that you have more energy to exercise more vigorously—for example, by walking further, breaking into a run, or adding a bike ride.

- ✓ **Concentrate** on activities that you enjoy. It doesn't matter what you do, as long as it keeps you moving. Examples are throwing a Frisbee with a dog or a buddy, walking laps around a mall window shopping, or cycling to the grocery store. Try a few different activities if you've never exercised before or aren't sure what you would enjoy. When you have a mood disorder, activities like gardening or working on a home improvement project can be fantastic methods to get you moving more—not only will they help you become more active, but they will also give you a feeling of purpose and accomplishment.

- ✓ **Be at ease**. Wear comfortable clothing and select a place that is both peaceful and energizing for you. A quiet nook of your home, a picturesque road, or your favorite city park could all be good options.

- ✓ **Reward yourself** for your efforts. Of course, part of the reward of finishing an exercise is how much better you'll feel afterward, but promising yourself an additional treat for exercising consistently increases your motivation. So, after a workout, treat yourself to a hot bubble bath, a great smoothie, or an extra episode of your favorite TV show.

- ✓ **Work-out in a group.** Exercising with a friend or loved one or even your children may make it more fun and pleasurable while motivating you to stay on an exercise plan. You'll also feel better than if you exercised on your own. In addition, a company might be just as beneficial as exercise when suffering from a mood disorder like depression.

Simple ways to get more exercise that doesn't need going to the gym

Don't you have a 30-minute slot set aside for yoga or a bike ride? Don't be concerned. Consider physical activity as a way of life rather than a task to cross off your to-do list. Examine your daily routine for opportunities to add action here, there, and everywhere.

- ✓ **Doing household chores:** Clean the house, wash the car, take care of the yard and garden, use a push mower to mow the lawn, and sweep the sidewalk or patio with a broom.

- ✓ **Workout on the go:** For example, instead of driving, ride your bike or walk to an appointment; take the stairs instead of the elevator; briskly walk to the bus stop and get off one stop early; park at the back of the lot and step inside the store or office, or go for a vigorous walk during your coffee break.

- ✓ **Fun with family**: Jog around the soccer field during your child's practice, incorporate a local bike ride into your weekend routine, play tag with your kids in the yard, go canoeing on a lake, or take your dog for a walk in a new location.

- ✓ **Use your imagination** to come up with exercise ideas. For example, pick fruit in an orchard, dance to music, go to the beach or on a stroll, stretch gently while watching TV, form an office bowling team, or enroll in a martial arts, dance, or yoga class.

Have you ever felt exhausted and unmotivated after a large meal or attempted to trudge through a meeting soon after lunch? If yes, then you would be aware that what you eat has a significant impact on your productivity and focus.

But it's much more than just being tired after a heavy dinner. The food you eat gives your body, including your brain and nervous system, the raw resources it needs to function. Surprisingly, our digestive system and our brain have a complex relationship.

It is critical to maintain attention and concentration throughout the day to be productive. There are various strategies to improve your attention (for example, becoming more conscious, developing your attention formula, beginning to include short naps throughout the day, etc.). Still, we frequently overlook that food plays a significant role in how we feel during the day. Although the brain only makes up 2% of an adult's weight, it consumes 20% of the energy produced by the body. Therefore, if you don't provide your brain the nourishment it needs, you'll experience several symptoms, including memory loss, weariness, and concentration issues.

Owing to meal composition, vitamin content, the impacts of different substances and constituents of food, or our gut health, what we eat can have a tremendous effect on our day-to-day productivity and focus, as well as our stress levels. Here are a few of the food elements that may have the most significant impact on mental health.

We'll go over the logic and reason behind why certain foods are necessary for good attention and concentration and why others should be avoided. There have been hundreds of studies on this subject, which back the reasons which will be shared as we proceed.

Macronutrients: A macronutrient is a term that translates to "big nutrients." Protein, carbohydrates, and fat are the three components that make up the most significant majority of our diets.

Protein is a nutrient that gives the body the building blocks to make new proteins, such as those found in muscles and other bodily parts. Meat, fish, eggs, beans, nuts, and seeds are all excellent sources of protein.

Carbs, short for carbohydrates, are natural sugars that produce energy. The best carbs to eat are fiber-complex carbs, such as vegetables, fruits, legumes, and whole grains.

Fat is the most calorie-dense food, and while it's acquired a poor rap over the years, it's vitally necessary for body (and brain) function. Meat and eggs, butter, oil, nuts, and seeds all contain fat.
Eating a healthy macronutrient balance is essential for ensuring that we have enough energy to go through the day and feel well enough to focus on our tasks.

If you eat too little protein and fat, your blood sugar levels will fluctuate, leaving you exhausted and "hungry" until your next meal.

You may feel lethargic all day if you eat too few carbs, as carbs provide quick-acting energy. Therefore, most people should acquire roughly 50% of their calories from carbohydrates, 30% from fat, and 20% from protein as a general rule of thumb.

Micronutrients: Micronutrients, on the other hand, are what we refer to as "tiny nutrients." These are the vitamins and minerals found in our meals. Vitamins and minerals play hundreds, if not thousands, of roles in the body, and the best way to make sure you're getting enough of them is to eat a varied, balanced diet.

B-vitamins, vitamin D, and magnesium are some micronutrients to consider when it comes to focus and stress. Getting enough of these nutrients can be as simple as eating a well-balanced, diverse meal and spending time in the sun.

Food's ingredients and biological components: Apart from macro-nutrients and micro-nutrients, various food elements or biological components also impact your productivity and focus.

Antioxidants are the plant chemicals that assist in preventing the build-up of dangerous free radicals, which are unstable chemicals that can cause inflammation and cell damage when they accumulate in large amounts, leading to chronic disease and stress. The term "antioxidant" comes from the term "free radical damage," which is also known as "oxidative stress."
Unfortunately, dietary intolerances like gluten intolerance, dairy intolerance, and intolerance to nightshade plants like

tomatoes can be a significant productivity stumbling block. If you have chronic heartburn, bloating, constipation, or diarrhea due to food intolerance, getting things done can be challenging and a continual cause of stress.

Gut-brain Axis: The "gut-brain axis," or the line of communication between your digestive system and your brain, is another critical component to consider. The gut-brain axis is "the bidirectional connection that happens between the gut and our central nervous system." It is the reason why we feel butterflies in our stomachs before giving a public speech or doing something that makes us uneasy. Depending on the ratios of healthy and harmful bacteria inhabiting your digestive system, the billions of bacteria in your gut may have a beneficial or destructive impact on your brain and central nervous system.

The bacteria in our gut may make and influence neurotransmitters in our brains, impacting brain health and mood. Changes in gut health have also been related to mental health issues like depression and anxiety. The gut also produces the bulk of serotonin, a 'feel-good' neurotransmitter that affects mood and digestion. In addition, fiber fermentation can cause the bacteria in the stomach to produce short-chain fatty acids (SCFAs), which can help with memory and learning. People with an unhealthy gut usually feel brain fog and fatigue due to faulty digestion or absorption of nutrients, inflammation, or metabolites of harmful bacteria, resulting in a loss of focus and productivity.

Essentials for a healthy gut: You can make four food modifications to maintain a healthy gut. Scientific study on the impacts of nutrition on cognitive performance backs up these four criteria.

✓ **Consumption of probiotics and fermented foods**: Fermented foods, such as yogurt, are excellent natural sources of probiotics, which are beneficial bacteria that can colonize your stomach. Include these foods in your diet to help rebalance the bacteria ratios in your gut, boosting the multiplication of healthy bacteria while crowding out the harmful bacteria that may be causing digestive problems.

Remember that gut bacteria aid in the production and effect of neurotransmitters, serotonin, and SCFAs, all of which can affect the brain. Therefore, a healthy mix of gut bacteria is critical for your overall health.

✓ **Eat a low inflammation diet:** Inflammation is the body's immune response to injury or illness, but it can be a problem if it becomes persistent. For example, chronic inflammation has been associated with type 2 diabetes, heart disease, and brain illnesses such as Alzheimer's.

An anti-inflammatory diet should target inflammation and free radical activity because inflammation and oxidative damage caused by free radicals frequently go hand in hand. Therefore, anti-inflammatory omega-3 fats from foods like fatty fish, chia seeds, and flax seeds should be included in the diet. It should also have a wide variety of antioxidant-rich fruits and vegetables.

Inflammatory foods should also be limited or avoided. Unfortunately, many foods in today's dietary environment induce inflammation. Some food items that are high in pro-inflammatory compounds that you should avoid:

- Sugars are added to sodas, snack cakes, cereals, desserts, and other foods
- Foods that have been highly processed, such as frozen and boxed meals and snacks
- Fast food

Sugar is a potent pro-inflammatory, and new research reveals that it may be more linked to heart disease than saturated fat and cholesterol.

- ✓ **Increase fiber consumption:** Fiber is prebiotic, which means it feeds the good bacteria in your stomach. SFC is created when these bacteria break down fiber, and they can aid memory and learn via the gut-brain axis.

  Fruits, vegetables, nuts, seeds, beans, and whole grains are all high in fiber. Best of all, increasing your fiber consumption from whole foods will improve your antioxidant consumption naturally. If you have constipation, fiber can help you get back on track.

- ✓ **Consume enough good fats:** Although fat was regarded initially as a dietary villain, it is no longer seen as such. The alleged association between dietary fat and heart disease was based on faulty research. New evidence reveals that dietary fat and cholesterol play a minor, if any, impact on heart disease. Fat is also necessary for proper brain function.

Superfoods to boost focus and concentration

Having seen the essential role of nutrition enhancing Focus and concentration, let's look at some of the food items at the top of the chart. Regular consumption of these foods has long-lasting effects on the functioning of our brain.

a) Water: Probably, one of the most vital but neglected elements of our daily diet is water. Drinking water and brain function are inextricably related, as is common knowledge. Lack of water in the brain can result in a range of symptoms:

- Difficulty in focusing and paying attention
- Brain exhaustion
- Fog in the head

- Aches and pains
- Disruptions in sleep
- Irritableness

Water makes about 85 percent of the brain. Water is required for all brain functions because it provides essential electrical energy. The brain consumes twice as much power as the rest of the body's cells, and water is the most efficient energy source. Water is also required to create neurotransmitters- dopamine and norepinephrine, which help executive function and hormones in the brain. Sufficient water consumption allows us to think 14 percent faster, stay concentrated for longer, and be more creative.

How much water to drink?

The recommended consumption is determined by factors such as sex, age, exercise level, etc. However, in general, people over the age of 19 should drink 3.7 liters per day (including everything they eat and drink) and 2.7 liters per day (including everything they eat and drink). So, this equates to approximately 13 cups of liquids for men while it equates to around 9 cups for women.

b) Blueberries: Studies have demonstrated blueberries to improve concentration and memory for up to 5 hours after consumption. Volunteers were given a blueberry smoothie in the morning, and their ability to do mental tasks was assessed in the afternoon. They discovered that those who drank the blueberry smoothie performed better on mental activities after 5 hours than those who didn't. Conversely, individuals who did not consume the blueberry drink reported a 15-20% decline in performance.

Antioxidants, vitamin C, vitamin E, and, most importantly, flavonoids abound in blueberries. When flavonoids are taken, they activate an enzyme that increases oxygen and blood flow to the brain, which helps with memory, focus, and learning new information.

c)Avocados: Avocados are powerhouses rich in beneficial fats and are genuinely a goldmine for nutrients that boost brain function, despite their reputation for being "too fatty." Certain nutrients can help with cognitive processes, including focus and memory in the brain. Avocados are abundant in various nutrients that help the brain in a variety of ways.

Avocados include 75 percent monounsaturated fats. Monounsaturated fats aid in the formation of acetylcholine, the neurotransmitter essential for memory and learning in the brain. They are also high in tyrosine, a dopamine precursor amino acid. This is the brain's feel-good neurotransmitter that keeps us focused and motivated. Both of these vitamins have neuroprotective characteristics that protect you from blood clots (as well as stroke), and they're beneficial at keeping your attention and memory sharp. Avocados also contain the highest protein and lowest sugar content of any fruit, as well as maintaining your blood sugar levels throughout the day.

d)Leafy greens: Someone who ate two daily portions of vegetables had the mental concentration of people five years their junior, according to research published in Neurology. Potassium is found in leafy green vegetables like spinach, which speeds up the connections between neurons in our brain, making it more responsive.

Lutein is abundant in green plants such as spinach and kale (leaf cabbage). Lutein is a pigment found in fruits and vegetables, a critical player in improving learning, memory, and preserving brain function. According to a study published in the journal Ageing Neuroscience, those with higher levels of lutein had 'younger' brains than their counterparts – in other words, their neural responses were similar to those of younger individuals.

Spinach is high in iron, which helps us maintain our energy levels throughout the day. It also contains vitamin B, which supports brain health by preventing free radicals and improving blood flow.

Kale is a nutritional powerhouse! It has about as much vitamin C as an orange and is a good source of vitamin B, which can help relieve stress, boost mood, and function as an antidepressant. It can also help to prevent memory loss and slow down the effects of aging in the brain.

e) Coffee: Caffeine and antioxidants, two primary components of coffee, are beneficial to your brain. It causes:

Increased alertness: Caffeine in coffee has a lot of favorable impacts on the brain. Caffeine keeps your brain awake by inhibiting adenosine, a sleep-inducing chemical messenger.
Improved mood: Caffeine may increase the levels of neurotransmitters that make you feel good, such as serotonin.
Sharpened concentration: One study found that individuals were more effective at tasks that needed attention when drinking one large coffee in the morning or in lesser quantities throughout the day.

f) Turmeric: This deep-yellow spice is a crucial component of curry powder and provides various brain-health benefits. The critical element in turmeric, curcumin, passes the blood-brain barrier, allowing it to enter the brain and benefit the cells.

It's an antioxidant and anti-inflammatory chemical that's been connected to a variety of cognitive advantages, including**:**

- ✓ Curcumin may assist persons with Alzheimer's disease to enhance their memory. It may also aid in the removal of amyloid plaques, which are a hallmark of Alzheimer's disease

- ✓ Depression is alleviated by increasing serotonin and dopamine levels, which both improve mood. Curcumin alleviated depressive symptoms just as well as an antidepressant in a six-week study
- ✓ Curcumin enhances brain-derived neurotrophic factor, a type of growth hormone that aids in creating new brain cells

g) Broccoli: Broccoli is high in antioxidants and other vital plant components. It also abounds in essential vitamin K. This fat-soluble vitamin is required to form sphingolipids, a type of fat found in dense concentration in brain cells. A higher vitamin K consumption has been associated with enhanced memory in older persons in a few trials. Aside from vitamin K, broccoli includes several anti-inflammatory and antioxidant substances that may help protect the brain from injury.

h) Pumpkin Seeds: Pumpkin seeds are high in antioxidants, which protect the body and brain from the effects of free radicals. In addition, magnesium, iron, zinc, and copper are all abundant in them. These nutrients are all essential for brain health. Zinc is a crucial component of nerve signaling. Many neurological disorders, such as Alzheimer's disease, depression, and Parkinson's disease, have been associated with zinc deficiency.

Magnesium is a mineral that is found in many foods. Magnesium is necessary for memory and learning. In addition, many neurological illnesses, such as migraines, depression, and epilepsy, are connected to low magnesium levels. Because seeds are high in these micronutrients, pumpkin seeds in your diet are likely to reap their benefits.

i) Dark Chocolate: Dark chocolate and cocoa powder are high in flavonoids, caffeine, and antioxidants, all of which are beneficial to the brain. Flavonoids are a class of plant-based antioxidants. Chocolate flavonoids concentrate on the parts of the brain that deal with learning and memory. These substances, according to researchers, may assist improve memory and slow down age-related mental deterioration.

According to research, people who ate chocolate more frequently fared better in many mental tasks, including those involving memory, than those who ate it less often, according to a study involving over 900 people. In addition, according to studies, chocolate is a proven mood enhancer.

j) Nuts: Nuts have been demonstrated in studies to improve measures of heart health, and a healthy heart is connected to a healthy brain. In addition, according to a 2014 study, nuts can aid boost memory and perhaps prevent neurodegenerative disorders.

Another critical study discovered that women who ate nuts regularly for several years had a better memory than those who did not. Nuts include several substances that may explain their brain-health benefits, including healthy fats, antioxidants, and vitamin E.

k) Oranges: One medium orange can provide you with all of the vitamin C you require for the day. Vitamin C is a critical element in preventing mental decline, therefore doing so is crucial for brain health.

According to a 2014 review article, eating enough vitamin C-rich foods can protect against age-related mental decline and Alzheimer's disease. Vitamin C is a potent antioxidant that aids in the battle against free radicals, harming brain cells. Vitamin C also helps to maintain brain health as you become older. Bell peppers, guava, kiwi, tomatoes, and strawberries all have high levels of vitamin C.

l)Eggs: Eggs are high in vitamins B6 and B12, folate, and choline, which are essential for brain function. Choline is a necessary component for the production of acetylcholine, a neurotransmitter that aids in mood and memory regulation. Higher choline consumption was associated with greater memory and mental performance in two studies. Because egg yolks are one of the most concentrated sources of choline, eating eggs is a simple way to get it.

m)Green Tea: Green tea's caffeine increases brain function in the same way that coffee does. It has been discovered to boost alertness, performance, memory, and focus. In addition, it contains additional components that make it a brain-healthy beverage.

L-theanine is an amino acid that can pass the blood-brain barrier and boost the activity of the neurotransmitter GABA, which helps you feel less anxious and relaxed. L-theanine also lets you relax without making you tired by increasing the frequency of alpha waves in your brain.

n) Fatty Fish: Fatty fish is generally at the top of the list when it comes to brain meals. Salmon, trout, and sardines are examples of this type of fish, all of which are high in omega-3 fatty acids. Fat makes up about 60% of your brain, with omega-3 fat accounting for half of that.Omega-3 fatty acids help your brain create brain and nerve cells, and they're also crucial for learning and memory. Omega-3 fatty acids have a few further advantages for your brain. For one thing, they may help prevent Alzheimer's disease by slowing age-related mental decline

How to Manage the External Environment for Focus?

Having mastered the internal factors impacting our ability to focus, let's look at how we can limit the interference from the external environment for greater focus.

The external environment is a mix of physical variables, consisting of our environment and the people we are surrounded with. We have already covered some prominent sources of distraction and their impact on focus in the previous chapter. Let's now look at the ways to control them.

1.Chatty Colleagues: If you're experiencing trouble with chatty or distracted team members, try having a private discussion with them about how it's affecting your day. Alternatively, if you have one, close your office door. If you need to be focused and concentrate, another option is to put on a pair of headphones

2.Noisy Workplace: If you have an office, the simplest thing you can do is close the door to give yourself some privacy and quiet time. Can you approach co-workers who you know are making a lot of noise and have a calm discussion about how their behaviors harm your ability to concentrate? Is it necessary for you to work at a desk? If you have a particular project that requires peaceful, uninterrupted time, consider working from a quiet space within your building. Working from home (if possible) or a different location, such as a park or café, are viable options.

3.Email Interruptions: Some of the most effective ways of controlling the mail menace and focus on what needs to be done are as under:

***Blocking off time*:** Set aside a set period to work on a project or job without interruption. Commit to not checking emails (or returning phone calls) during this time.

Offline method of operation: Set your PC or laptop to offline mode and wait until you're ready to respond to email messages in your inbox. Allow emails to pile instead of examining and responding to them one at a time. Then set aside focused time to review and respond to the emails. It will take less time to respond to emails in bulk than it will to respond to them one at a time, and it will help you keep focused on the project at hand without getting side-tracked.

Interval checking: To ensure you are completely caught up, one technique is to check your emails two or three times a day — in the morning, at lunchtime, and an hour before you leave. It's a good idea to design an out-of-office message if you decide to use this strategy.

Don't check your e-mail first thing in the morning: This strategy may be tough to adapt depending on your circumstances, but you will be far more productive if you can. Rather than checking email first thing in the morning, use this time to work on your one or two top goals for the day when you are more motivated and focused.

4.Smartphone: Even if we're working on a critical job, it's all too easy to check our phones. What is the solution? Put your phone in a drawer or put it out of reach so you won't be tempted to glance at it. Another effective way is to disable notifications. Turn off all notifications that don't need to be answered right away, mainly social media notifications. Make some alerts mute and hide them from your lock screen if they're insignificant.

5.Social media: Set specified timeframes or limitations for checking social media, much like you do with your smartphone and email. Ensure all notifications are turned off when you need to spend concentrated, productive time on a topic or project.

a) Turn off all of your push notifications for one hour before bed and one hour after waking up.

b) When you're working, put your phone in a drawer.

c) Only check social media on one device.

d) Set aside 30 minutes each day to stay connected.

e) Set aside one hour each day to respond to emails.

f) Use RSS or Email to subscribe to your favorite websites.

g).Post on social media Using third-party applications

6.Meetings: According to a TED study, a third of that time is wasted on ineffective meetings. According to a Clarizen survey, workers consider meetings as a waste of time. Here are ten ways that leaders and managers can begin holding productive and effective team meetings that benefit everyone involved:

Set a positive tone for each meeting: A fantastic beginning point for getting everyone in the room in a good mindset and invigorated for the conference is to have everyone share something they've made progress on or are pleased about. This immediately establishes the tone and focus of the meeting. As a result, people arrive from positive contribution and positivity rather than negativity about attending the conference.

There should be a clear leader in the room: Whatever the meeting's goal, someone in the room must take leadership in directing and guiding it. This individual will set the agenda for the meeting, ensure that it stays on topic, and keep it within the agreed-upon timeline. In addition, they will frequently update attendees on progress, clarify what has to be done after the conference, and obtain a commitment from attendees on future next steps. People with the most significant personalities or extensive ideas might dominate and prevent softer characters from contributing if no one takes control.

Ensure that the right people are in the room: Consider the last fantastic meeting you attended. Was the session jam-packed with folks "making up the numbers," or was it jam-packed with people who were contributing and providing input? Take time to examine who will be involved to host a genuinely beneficial meeting. You want people in the room who will offer value, be active contributors, have background knowledge, make decisions, take action, and be directly affected by the meeting's outcome.

If you don't have to, avoid overcrowding the room with people there for the sake of status or a fear of missing out on something. Instead of bringing in passive onlookers, focus on bringing in people who add value to the meeting. If you have the freedom to schedule your appointments whenever you want, focus on making them as productive as possible. In various sessions, make use of people's strengths.

Not everyone on your team or in your company is a good match for every meeting. Getting clear on what meetings team members should and should not be a part of is a piece of beautiful advice for generating productive meetings. Don't just invite people you believe will contribute the most; instead, ask those you know will make the most difference. Each of us has our own set of skills. Some members of your team will thrive in brainstorming sessions, while others may become anxious at the prospect of participation.

The same can be said for status and process meetings. When making the most of a forum, think about the type of vibe you want in the room and who can contribute the most value to the table. If you've figured it out, make sure the correct individuals are in the room. Being the conductor of a great orchestra is sometimes compared to leading fruitful meetings. The result might be a major disaster if you don't have the correct complementing instruments and performers in the room, collaborating and working in harmony. The effects, though, can be stunning and motivating if the appropriate artists are brought together.

Define clear action steps and responsibilities at the end of meetings: Consider the last meeting you attended; chances are you had a lot of exciting talks, as well as valuable ideas and thoughts. But what happened at the meeting's conclusion? Were there clear action steps and duties outlined, or did you all go your separate ways? Setting aside time at the end of each meeting for everyone to offer their most crucial insight is valuable.

This encourages participation and collaboration and guarantees that everyone leaves the meeting with a clear understanding of the meeting's worth to emphasize this point. The meeting's leader must explicitly set out the action steps, personal responsibilities, and timelines for taking action on the meeting's essential parts.

Make the meeting's purpose crystal clear: One of the most challenging aspects of holding a good and productive meeting is staying on course. This is because many meetings are born without a clear goal or even a plan.

Some meetings take place solely because someone has decided that a weekly status meeting will be held. Attending conferences like this without explicit knowledge of what the meeting is about, what the plan is, or the meeting's priorities might make you feel like the meeting is a waste of time. On the other hand, you will be more involved, know what to prepare ahead of time, and see the meeting's expected results if you are clear on the meeting's goal.

Reduce the length of meetings: You should know how long the session should last if you have a clear objective and agenda. Many of the conferences I've attended in the past were scheduled for 45 minutes or 60 minutes. Some sessions ended earlier than expected, but the meeting continued for no apparent reason because the time frame had been specified for a specific period. Start scheduling appointments with a shorter time frame, such as 30 or 40 minutes, and observe if they become more productive and efficient.

On-Time begin and end: No one wants to be kept waiting for meetings to start and then have to reschedule if they go late. Participants know what to anticipate and arrive on time if you hold meetings that begin and end on time. If team members fail to appear on time, a second meeting with that person may be necessary to clarify that you expect them to appear on time.

Modify the environment: If your meetings take too long to get started or are becoming stale, it may be time to switch things up. For example, I've had some of my most productive meetings just by getting out of the office and traveling to an inspiring location or by holding a session or two at a nearby park.

7.Multi-Tasking: Multitasking causes us to become less focused, energetic, and productive. This is because our brains are simply incapable of handling many activities at the same time. Work in time blocks. It reduces the amount of distraction that our increasingly linked lifestyles are subjected to. It shields us not just from external distractions but also from self-inflicted distractions.

Setting aside an intended amount of time for specific projects or tasks and making a deliberate effort to avoid distractions or interjections from others is known as time blocking. After that block of time has passed, take a planned break before starting the following focused time block. Each full-time block is devoted to a single task/project or a group of related tasks. I use the 60-60-30 method for time blocking: Take a 10-minute break after 50 minutes of work. Next, work for another 50 minutes before taking a ten-minute break. Then take 30 minutes to refuel, which could include eating lunch, going for a stroll, or doing something else. To help you work in blocks of time, use the Pomodoro Technique.

8.Micro-management: For managers, relinquishing some control is never easy. However, it would help if you delegated authority to your team. It doesn't imply you should thoroughly check out if you're not a micromanager. It entails keeping an eye on everyone and mentoring them throughout the day without interfering with their work.

Tips to get rid of micro-management:

Get used to delegating*:* You could unwittingly micromanage your team if you don't know how to trust successfully. Allocating assignments that play to each employee's skills and aspirations while also learning and growing in their roles is critical.

According to a Gallup study, CEOs who are good at delegating produce 33% more revenue. In addition, these executives empower their staff and increase their morale by yielding some responsibility, all while freeing up their time to focus on tasks that will deliver the best results for the firm. When delegating, remember that you shouldn't instruct your coworker on completing a project step by step; it's micromanaging. Instead, concentrate on the desired outcome and ensure they have the necessary resources, training, and authority to achieve it.

Establish clear goals: You'll set your team up for failure if you don't set expectations upfront. Likewise, your staff will perform better if you are explicit about the objectives of an assigned project when it has to be completed and the benchmarks you will use to gauge its success.

Some bosses micromanage because they believe they are the only ones who can properly execute a task—before even trying to explain it to someone else. Instead, allow your personnel to demonstrate their abilities by clearly stating the objectives of a specific effort and how they relate to the organization's mission. But, again, it's worth repeating: You're telling them what you want them to accomplish, not how you anticipate them to achieve it.

Forget about being perfect: There are numerous approaches to completing a job or assignment. It will be easier to cease micromanaging if you grasp this as soon as possible. Allow your staff to test fresh ways to an issue by allowing them to experiment with their ideas. Accept failure. Your team will stagnate if you routinely repeat and reward the concept, "It's always been done this way." Encourage innovation and be prepared for any accidents that may occur due to allowing your personnel to attempt new things. Consider a project that doesn't go as planned as a learning opportunity and a lesson for the future. You'll be less likely to micromanage your team if you're open to fresh ideas and let go of perfectionism.

Employ the correct personnel: This may seem self-evident, but you must recruit the appropriate individuals. You're more inclined to micromanage someone who is unqualified for a position or has the necessary skills. A monetary penalty accompanies every bad hire: According to a poll conducted by the Society of Human Resource Management, the average cost-per-hire is $4,129. The average time to fill a position is 42 days. That's a lot of time for other employees to pick up the slack for someone you just fired, and it could hurt general productivity and morale.

Find out how your employees prefer to be managed: If you want to build a solid bond with your team, find out how each person desires to be managed. For example, some employees may claim they don't mind a little more hand-holding, but you're more likely to hear that they value trust and autonomy.

By holding this two-way conversation, you show your employees that you appreciate their input while also letting go of any preconceived notions you may have about how you're doing as a boss. On the other hand, you could be ignoring red flags indicating you're a micromanager.

These suggestions do not imply that you should delegate all of your jobs to your staff or that you should cease checking in and providing feedback. Establish open communication routes and let your team know you'll be there when they need you.

However, avoid being there when you aren't required. Instead, allow your employees to experiment, learn, and grow. Then, you can put your faith in their judgment, talents, and knowledge. Your role as a manager is to stay focused on the broader picture rather than getting mired down in the details and micromanaging.

9.Cluttered workplace: It's also reasonably common for businesspeople to have messy offices with various photos, books, a messy desk, and an always-on flat panel on the wall. A cluttered work environment equals a cluttered mind. Remove unneeded clutter from your office to help you focus better. Sure, you can display some family photos and souvenirs in your office to make it a more welcoming place to work. At the same time, get rid of anything that doesn't serve a specific job purpose, as well as the "junk" that has gathered on your desk and shelves over time. Maintain a tidy and well-organized workspace. Get rid of anything you don't need. Documents should be filed in the proper folders. To reduce the number of filing cabinets, you should put as much paperwork as possible in the cloud. Ensure that all office supplies have a place to go and that they are returned at the end of the day. Even if you don't do it every day, you should clean your desk at least once a week.

10.Lighting: You may already know how lighting influences productivity without having to read a scientific study. Bright lights can be too harsh at times, and staring at the blue light of a computer for an extended period might strain your eyes. Certain sorts of light, you see, will set off our body's circadian rhythm. In other words, it can elicit particular responses such as the urge to sleep, relax, or be stimulated. Certain types of illumination can even help to alleviate sadness by boosting mood, energy, and alertness. When constructing a workspace, these considerations must be taken into account.

Artificial illumination is nearly impossible to avoid in the office. However, depending on the work being done, it's critical to evaluate the sort of lighting you utilize. In addition, it's crucial to have an accurate lighting source in a workplace where computers are frequently used to reduce the strain on workers' eyes caused by the brightness of the computer screen.

Artificial lighting can be bright or low, affecting employees differently: Dim lighting puts undue strain on the eyes, leading to vision problems or headaches. In addition, employees may become drowsy or lose their motivation, resulting in a drop in total productivity.

Bright or high-intensity lights can harm productivity. In addition, fluorescent or halogen lighting can give workers headaches; too bright lighting has been identified as one of the leading causes of migraines in workers. In an office, it's critical to strike a good balance between dim and bright illumination.

Using natural light: Natural lighting is one of the best sources of lighting for a workspace. Direct sunlight can lessen the frequency of headaches in workers, as well as tension and tiredness. Window access and natural illumination are two characteristics that might boost employee happiness while lowering anxiety levels. In addition, natural light improves workers' vision, reducing eye strain.

Lighting suggestions for your workspace: According to the American Society of Interior Design research, 68 percent of workers are unhappy with their office lighting. To offer the best environment for your employees, it's critical to strike a balance between artificial and natural illumination in the office. Create lighting for your workstation that meets the demands of both your area and your staff.

Warm lighting is ideal for private spaces such as break rooms. It can induce feelings of relaxation and contentment. The adequate lighting for conference rooms is mid-toned lighting. It's more inviting yet still cool enough to keep you awake. For brainstorming areas, cool lighting is ideal. This light has the potential to boost alertness, happiness, and productivity. It can also alleviate fatigue by lowering melatonin levels.

11.Temperature: According to the findings, temperature affects pupil attention span. Students in both the more relaxed and warmer rooms poorly performed on tests than those in the control room kept at a constant temperature of roughly 70 degrees. A comparable study conducted at Cornell University found that the ideal temperature is between 70 and 78 degrees. This study continues its investigation into why climate change may have such a significant impact. The unpleasantness of your surroundings isn't the only factor affecting your memory and learning ability. Your mind becomes preoccupied with managing body temperature, either cooling or heating, in an overly cold or overly hot setting, detracting from your concentration. Warm environments might make you sleepy and fatigued. Colder climates may provide a jolt of energy to help you wake up, but your body is forced to spend that energy to keep you warm.

With this, we conclude this section on mastering the focus. In the final chapter, we will merge all the learnings to design a custom action plan for you. Finish the assignments and join me there.

Chapter 4: Synopsis

Focus is essentially a muscle. So, if you're wondering how to focus better, it's a skill that must be practiced regularly. That means you'll have to work hard to avoid checking your phone every two minutes if you want to finish that project.

Most people can't concentrate for two reasons:

1. We are never taught how to concentrate.
2. We don't practice concentration.

To become a focus expert, it's essential to understand the mind. Once we know it, we can control it. Once we can manage it, we can master the focus.

There are two critical things to learn concentration:

- Awareness
- Mind

Consider awareness as the glowing ball of light and mind as the vast field with various chambers. Each chamber is occupied by emotions like anger, jealousy, hunger, greed, sex, joy, happiness, etc. The glowing ball of self-awareness can travel to any area of mind and illuminate it. Whichever room it lights up, we become conscious of it, and the awareness goes up.

Concentration requires keeping the awareness of one particular area for an extended period.

How to practice concentration?

One of the best ways is to allow awareness to remain on one thing for a long duration. So, keep looking for such opportunities throughout the day. For example, while talking to your spouse, partner, friend, or family member, imagine keeping the ball of awareness on them and giving them undivided attention. That's the best way to practice.

To focus on the present, it's imperative to get rid of these worries about the future and calm yourself.

Focus is choosing the proper thought among thousands of ideas going in our minds. To do so, a few simple steps may help:

1.Learn to distinguish between disturbing and non-disturbing thoughts. One non-disturbing thought can knock off all the troubling thoughts and bring you back to focus.
2.Constantly being worried about the goal or what we want to achieve shifts focus to the future and drifts us away from the present. Unless we work on what we are good at and remain focused on the present, it's impossible to achieve the future goal.
3. Replace To do list with Not-To-Do List. This implies preparing a list of all the stuff, which you are not supposed to do.

Mastering the focus requires control of self and managing the external environment. Therefore, we will be covering the how part of the focus in three segments:

- How to train the mind?
- How to train the body?
- How to manage the environment?

How to train the mind?

Essential methods & techniques that can be used to train the mind to focus better are:
1.Mindfulness

2.Meditation
3.Sleep
4.Exercising the brain

1.Mindfulness: The ability to be fully present, aware of where we are and what we're doing, and not unduly reactive or overwhelmed by what's going on around us is known as mindfulness.

Key Benefits Of Mindfulness

- ✓ Memory Enhancement
- ✓ Meta-cognitive Awareness
- ✓ Reduced Anxiety
- ✓ Low Emotional Reactivity
- ✓ Visual Attention Processing
- ✓ Stress Reduction
- ✓ Reduction in Physical Pain

Group-based Mindfulness Techniques

- **Mindfulness-Based Stress Reduction (MBSR):** It is a group technique that emphasizes yoga, meditation, and other similar activities.

- **Mindfulness-Based Cognitive Therapy (MBCT):** Mindful breathing and meditation are used in MBCT.It focuses on teaching techniques to reframe feelings and not eradicating them.

Common mindfulness techniques

- **Focussed attention on the breath**: It cultivates present mindedness by focussing on the breath movement.

- **Open awareness**: It promotes staying focused on the present moment by being aware of the surroundings. Paying attention to the objects in your vicinity and sensation from the various elements can help to relax and cleanse the mind.

Illustrations for practicing mindfulness in daily activities:

a) Walking: Notice the rhythm of each step, feel the breeze, listen to noises, savor the colors. Attention to all these elements helps to focus on the present.

b) Interactions: During conversations, listen with an open mind. Avoid being judgemental in arguments. Refrain from digging out the past instances; concentrate on the current situation only.

c) Public appearances: To reduce the stress before a public appearance, reflect on the feelings. Accept the feelings and remind yourself that these are momentary emotions and do not necessarily define you. Feel the muscles as they relax.

Mindfulness Tips:

1. Mindful Breathing
2. Engagement in the Task
3. Savour the process
4. Do Nothing
5. Rewind
6. Be mindful of the cognitive process
7. Sef-consciousness
8. Heightened awareness
9. Immersion in nature
10. Observe the drift

2.Meditation: It is a series of techniques designed to promote heightened awareness and focused concentration. It offers numerous psychological advantages and can also be used as a form of psychotherapy.

Concepts for practicing meditation:

1.Choose a peaceful place
2.Choose a short duration session of 5 to or 10 min, to begin with
3.Choose a comfortable body posture
4.Focus on your breath and pay attention to each sensation while breathing
5.Notice your thoughts, and whenever the mind wanders, concentrate on your breath

Forms of Meditation

1.Concentrative meditation: Requires to focus on a single item while phasing out everything else. Choose what to focus on-breath, word, or a mantra.

Steps involved

1) Choose the Target
2) Choose a position
3) Get into a relaxed state
4) Pay attention to the target
5) Stop self-talk
6) Eliminate the fear of failure

2.Mindfulness meditation: It relaxes the mind and body by slowing down the speed of thoughts. It involves deep breathing and awareness of the body and mind.

Mindfulness-based stress reduction and mindfulness-based cognitive therapy are examples of mindfulness meditation. Being aware and active in the present moment and self-acceptance are the main objectives.

Steps involved

1) Choose a comfortable position
2) Set a timer
3) Notice your breathing
4) Notice your thoughts
5) Take a break

Tips for practicing mindfulness meditation in daily routine:

- ✓ Brushing the teeth
- ✓ Dishwashing
- ✓ Washing clothes
- ✓ Driving
- ✓ Working out
- ✓ Getting kids to sleep

How meditation improves focus?

It improves brain structure by rewiring neural circuits. As a result, most-used connections are strengthened, and the least used ones are weeded off.

Meditation improves the volume of the brain region, which is crucial for memory & information retention. Regular meditation also reduces the size of the amygdala, a brain area involved in processing negative emotions like fear.

3.Sleep: Sleep permits the brain and body to settle down and engage in healing processes, which helps in the improvement of physical and mental performance. Lack of sleep disrupts the essential functions which affect thinking, concentration, energy levels, and mood.

According to brain plasticity theory, sleep permits neurons to restructure. As a result, it helps in clearing harmful by-products from the brain.

Key benefits of sleep:

- ✓ Improved brain efficiency
- ✓ The clarity to comprehend information
- ✓ Memory retention
- ✓ Alleviates Creativity
- ✓ Flushing out toxins from the brain

4.Brain exercises to strengthen focus: Focus is like a muscle. Exercising the brain regularly is essential for sustained concentration and focus. Brain exercises to sharpen the focus:

- ✓ Solve puzzles
- ✓ Card Games
- ✓ Building Vocabulary
- ✓ Leveraging senses
- ✓ Learn a skill
- ✓ Teach a skill
- ✓ Play or listen to music
- ✓ Explore variety in the routine
- ✓ Learn a new language
- ✓ Concentrate on others

How to train the body to focus?

The two main elements which play a vital role in preparing the body and improving concentration are:

1.Exercise
2.Nutrition

1.Exercise: Regular workout makes you feel more energetic, ensures better sleep, creates better memories, generates positive emotions, and relaxes your brain.

Crucial benefits of regular exercise:

- ✓ Enhanced energy
- ✓ Enhanced mood
- ✓ Defends against illnesses
- ✓ Improved memory, cognition, and learning

It also helps as an effective cure against mental health conditions:

- ➢ **Depression**: Physical activity causes the brain to release endorphins, which make you feel happy. It also helps in diverting attention and breaking the loop of negative thoughts.
- ➢ **Anxiety**: The release of endorphins relieves tension and stress and improves overall well-being.
- ➢ **Stress**: Exercise helps relax the muscles by releasing tension in the body and producing endorphins in the brain.
- ➢ **ADHD**: Raise in neurotransmitters like dopamine, norepinephrine, and serotonin levels while exercising aids in focus and attention.
- ➢ **Trauma**: Focussing on the body while exercising frees the nervous system and eliminates immobility stress associated with trauma. Cross-movement exercises that work both arms and legs work the best.

Tips for beginning with physical activity:

- ✓ Start small
- ✓ Workout in a high energy state
- ✓ Concentrate

- ✓ Be at ease
- ✓ Reward yourself
- ✓ Work out in groups

How to work out without going to the gym?

- ✓ Doing household chores
- ✓ Workout on the go
- ✓ Fun with the family
- ✓ Use your imagination

2.Nutrition: Food provides raw resources required for the correct functioning of the nervous system, mind, and body. The Digestive system and brain have a complex relationship. Nutrition is vital to provide the nourishment required for the healthy functioning of the body and mind.

- Macronutrients are also known as big nutrients. These include protein, fats, and carbohydrates. Balanced meals comprising 50% carbs,30% fats, and 20% protein are good to go.

- Micronutrients are the vitamins and minerals found in our meals. B Vitamins, Vitamin D, and magnesium are the micronutrients essential for focus.

In addition to macro and micronutrients, there are some other elements impacting focus and productivity.

Antioxidants: These are the plant chemicals, which prevent the accumulation of dangerous free radicals. Free radicals cause inflammation and may damage brain cells.

Gut-brain axis: it is the line of communication between the brain and digestive system. It is the bidirectional connection that happens between the gut and central nervous system. The healthy and harmful bacteria ratio determines the positive or negative impact on the brain and central nervous system. Unhealthy balance causes brain fog, fatigue, loss of focus, and productivity.

Essentials for a healthy gut:

- ✓ Probiotics and fermented foods: Fermented foods like yogurt provide healthy bacteria, which helps in keeping digestive problems at bay.

- ✓ Eating a low inflammation diet: Inflammation is associated with brain illness disease like Alzheimer's. Foods like fatty fish, chia seeds, flax seeds are rich in anti-inflammatory omega-3 fats, which counter the free radical activity and control inflammation.

- ✓ High fiber consumption: Fiber is pre-biotic; it feeds the good bacteria in the stomach. Fruits, vegetables, nuts, seeds, beans are all high in fiber.

- ✓ Consume good fats: It helps in healthy brain functioning.

Superfoods to boost focus and concentration

a) Water: It is required for all brain functions because it provides essential electrical energy. Lack of water in the brain can result in:

- Difficulty in focusing and paying attention
- Brain exhaustion
- Fog in the head
- Aches and pains
- Sleep disruptions
- Irritableness

b) Blueberries: It improves concentration and memory by increasing oxygen and blood flow to the brain. In addition, it is rich in antioxidants, vitamin c, vitamin E, and flavonoids.

c).Avocados: These are rich in healthy fats and other essential nutrients that boost brain function. In addition, avocados have high protein content and the lowest sugar content.

d).Leafy Greens: These are rich in potassium which speeds up the connections between neurons, making them more responsive. Lutein is also abundant in green plants such as spinach and kale. It improves learning, memory and preserves brain function.

e) Coffee: Caffeine and antioxidants, the two main components of coffee, cause increased alertness, improve mood and sharpen concentration.

f) Turmeric: Curcumin is the critical element in turmeric, passing the blood-brain barrier and benefiting brain cells.

g) Broccoli: It is high in antioxidants, vitamin k, and other vital plant components beneficial for enhanced memory functions.

h).Pumpkin Seeds: These are high in antioxidants, which protect the body and brain from the effects of free radicals. Magnesium, iron, zinc, and copper are the other brain health minerals found in abundant quantities.

i)Dark Chocolate: Contains flavonoids that help in learning and memory functions.

j) Nuts: These are rich in healthy fats, antioxidants, and vitamin E required for healthy heart function and boost memory.

k) Oranges: One medium-size orange can suffice the vitamin C requirement for a whole day. Vitamin C is critical for maintaining mental health.

l)Eggs: Eggs are rich in vitamins B6 and B12, which are vital for healthy brain function.

m)Green Tea: The presence of caffeine boosts alertness, performance, memory, and focus.

n) Fatty Fish: Salmon, trout, and sardines are examples of fatty fish. These are rich in omega-3 fatty acids, which are required for the smooth functioning of the brain.

How to manage the external environment?

The external environment includes the physical environment we live in and the people we are surrounded with. The prominent sources of distraction and the effective ways of dealing with external environmental factors can be summarized as under:

1)Chatty colleagues: Have a one-to-one discussion or close the door when engaged in deep work.

2)Noisy workplace: Cut the noise by either closing the door, shifting your workplace, putting on the headphones, or working from home.

3)Email interruptions: Effective ways of tackling it include:

- ✓ Blocking off time to check mails
- ✓ Offline method of operation
- ✓ Interval checking
- ✓ Avoid starting the day with emails.

4)Smartphone: Put your phone out of your reach so that you can concentrate on your task and do away with the temptation of checking it every few minutes.

5)Social media: Set specified timelines for checking social media. Turn off all notifications to avoid being distracted.

6)Meetings: Ten ways to avoid wasting time and conducting productive meetings:

- ✓ Set a positive tone for each meeting
- ✓ Appoint a clear leader to drive the agenda
- ✓ Only the required participants should be present for the meeting
- ✓ Define clear action steps at the end
- ✓ Make the meeting's agenda crystal clear
- ✓ Ensure that meetings are of optimum length only
- ✓ Begin and end in time
- ✓ Align the environment

7)Multi-Tasking: Using time blocks to focus on one task at a time helps to overcome it.60-60-30 method of time blocking and Pomodoro technique can be used to overcome it.

8)Micro-management: Tips to get rid of micro-management:

- ✓ Delegation
- ✓ Establish clear goals
- ✓ Quit perfection
- ✓ Employ the correct personnel
- ✓ Ask employee preference for supervision

9)Cluttered Work Place: A chaotic work environment resembles a disorganized mind and obstructs focus. Removing unwanted clutter and mess creates a positive work environment, making it easier to focus.

10)Lighting: Certain sorts of lights elicit particular responses, such as the urge to sleep, relax, or be stimulated. The right kind of lighting boosts the mood, enhances energy and alertness.

11)Temperature: Temperature affects pupil attention span. The ideal climate, which aids concentration and focussing ability, is between 70-78 degrees.

Assignment 5

---

1. List down techniques, which you would be using to train your mind to focus.

2. How will you train your body to sharpen the concentration? Share the action points.

3.Share the action points to help you overcome external environment distractions at your workplace.

CHAPTER 5

Focus To Fortune Blueprint

"Focussing on things you can change, will change the things you can't."

-Lalit Hundalani

In the preceding chapters, we have covered almost all aspects of focus, including:

- ✓ What is Focus?
- ✓ Why is Focus important in life?
- ✓ Why is it challenging to Focus?
- ✓ How to Master the Focus?

Having covered these points in detail, we have got a fair understanding & knowledge of all that needs to be known, which is good.

This section will integrate all the knowledge and information to design the personalized blueprint for customized you.

The blueprint comprises of below steps:

1. Know Your-Self
2. Identify your Goal
3. Train the Brain
4. Train the body
5. Align the environment to get rid of distractions
6. Design a schedule
7. Get into action
8. Review the Progress
9. Do the course correction if required.
10. Persist & repeat

1. Know Yourself

The first step of the process is self-discovery. We live in the information age, where we have access to the entire world at our fingertips. As a result, we are always interested in what is going on in our community and around the globe. It's debatable if such a multitude of news is genuinely valuable for us, but the fact remains that we want to be aware of everything that is going on around us. It's ironic, in this situation, how little we know about ourselves. Lack of self-awareness is the primary source of discontent and dissatisfaction in most people I see, meet, or know.

Due to a lack of awareness, we continue to blame others for our shortcomings. We blame people, events, and circumstances, in fact, anything and everything except ourselves. The external emphasis does no help for us and only adds to our frustration. We have minimal influence over the outer world, so why invest time and energy there? Instead, why not concentrate on ourselves, become more self-aware, and explore how to gain the necessary life skills and improve our coping abilities?

Knowing self provides clarity to questions like:

- What forms our core?
- What drives us?
- What motivates us?
- What gets us going?
- Why do we feel the way we do?
- What is it that we are seeking?

Reduce distractions, set aside more time for yourself, and become more conscious of your inner self. Once you've done that, you'll better understand your foundation and the answers to the questions listed above.

2.Identify your Goal

Having a goal or an outcome provides clarity of purpose to progress in life.

Earl Nightingale famously stated in his now-legendary audiotape "The Strangest Secret" in the 1950s that 95% of people do not attain success in life simply because they do not have goals. He also said, "You become what you think about. If you think nothing, you become nothing". This is a powerful and direct statement. It makes it quite clear that the choices and decisions you make today will determine your future tomorrow.

Self-awareness (Step 1) allows us to identify the core quality or value which defines us and is intrinsic to our personality. We must ensure that our outcome is aligned with it.

Set your ultimate end goals, break them down into sub-goals with clear-cut timelines, and go about them one step at a time. I know it's not easy, but anything worth doing is not easy. It requires considerable effort, but in the end, it's worth it.

Once you have your goal plan or goal sheet in front of you, following the process becomes more straightforward. Read or write them daily so that you get a sense of direction and don't forget. Remember the old adage, **"Out of sight is out of mind."**

3.Train the Brain

In the preceding sections, we have covered in detail the critical role played by our mind in focus and concentration. Conditioning the mind to focus on what we want to achieve is a must. As you embark on this journey, there would be distractions galore. A trained brain is better equipped to

overcome these obstructions and keep moving. At any point in time, we have several negative
thoughts hovering in our minds, which stop us from taking action and make it difficult to persist in the face of adversity. The negative inner voice keeps on reminding:

- Why we can't do something
- What is not good about a situation
- Why we are not good enough
- Our past failures
- People can't be trusted
- What's not good around us
- Justifying our inaction
- Judging people
- Blaming others
- Spending time in the past
- Worrying about future
- Thinking about our Insecurities
- Lack of money
- Lack of time

These are examples of self-doubts that lead to mind wandering and make it difficult to focus on our outcomes. We fail to persist once we lose focus; we don't achieve what we aspire to if we don't persist.

The good news is that we can control our minds and change this behavior. In the earlier chapters, we have covered at length the mind, its vagaries, and the means of control. Any combination of the techniques mentioned in the section,

"How to master the Focus," can be utilized to train the mind.

Recap of mind training techniques:

1) Practicing Mindfulness
2) Practicing Meditation
3) Sleep
4) Brain Exercises

The application of mind training techniques allows better control, removes negative thoughts and negative emotions, and limits mind wandering to focus on our outcome single-mindedly.
Most of all, it allows changing the self-talk. Changing the self-talk leads to the formation of a positive belief system:

- Why I can't do it is replaced by How can I do it?
- This is not going to work becomes I will make it work.
- I can't afford it becomes how I can afford it?
- Scarcity is replaced by abundance.
- I don't have time is replaced by how can I prioritize better

Once that happens, you'll feel unstoppable and ready to go.

4.Train the body

Howsoever hard one may try, if you are not in the best of your health, you can't focus and aim high. A low state of health makes the accomplishment of even the mundane jobs an arduous task. We are all aware that a healthy mind resides in a healthy body. A healthy & fit body makes us feel energetic and much more committed. Any worthwhile goal requires considerable effort. To retain the focus for long hours and work consistently becomes more manageable if you are in the best of your health and vice-versa. Beyond fitness, physical health also helps get rid of physical and mental ailments, which helps lead a disease-free life. For these reasons, along with mind training, the body is equally important. As discussed in the earlier chapter, two essential elements of a healthy & disease-free life are:

1.Regular Exercise
2.Nutritious diet

Choose an exercise routine, which goes with your personality and lifestyle depending upon your age, weight, and nature of work. Just keep in mind that you need to choose something which you can stick to for a long. It should not be a one-day affair with fitness, rather a long-lasting, sustainable relationship. Something similar to marriage. There is a lot of information already available on this subject. For further details, you may consult an expert for a customized plan.
Along with exercise, diet plays a crucial role in keeping the mental faculties awake & supercharge the brain alertness levels. We have already covered the essential nutrients and the role of each one in improving our health and concentration, along with some of the brain superfoods.

Make your personalized diet plan, taking into account your calorie requirement and medical conditions, if any. Take expert advice if needed. Just a tiny caveat, don't starve yourself or go overboard. It must be an optimum diet plan to keep you alert, focussed, and energetic for the more significant part of the day.

Having frozen your diet and workout plan, time to move on and fix the surroundings.

5.Align the Environment

You have trained the mind and body, which is 80% of the stuff. Now you have internal controls in place; the next step requires cutting the distractions that interfere with you and don't focus.
Distractions can broadly be classified into two broad categories:

1.Physical environment
2.People

The physical environment comprises the workplace, infrastructure, noise, electronic gadgets, temperature, light, etc. People include your colleagues in the workplace. If it is work from home, then your family members as well. While choosing the work environment, be mindful of all the above elements. The purpose is to have minimal distractions so that the flow is not disturbed, and you can work without interruptions for long hours. Use the relevant tips & techniques shared in**," How to Master the Focus"** section & apply them at your workplace to eliminate distractions from offline & online sources.

The end goal is to design a work environment, which aids concentration and focus, not excuses.

6.Define a Schedule

By now, you have enough knowledge on what all needs to be done. But you just can't rely on the willpower to take you through daily. That's where daily routine or habits come into play. Use your will to form patterns. Once you have your schedule in place and habits are formed, reliance on willpower may come down. The schedule includes the tasks to be performed on a daily, weekly, fortnightly basis. Exercising the mind & body via mindfulness, meditation, physical workout, diet, etc., are part of the daily routine.

Reviewing the progress towards defined outcomes is a part of the weekly schedule.

Decluttering your workplace can be a weekly or fortnightly activity.

Setting up the workplace can be a part of the monthly routine.

Once identified what needs to be done, the bottom line is to put all the activities in a schedule by calendarizing them day-wise and assigning time slots.

This way, you will ensure that things happen as planned & don't merely remain on paper or in your thoughts.

7.Just do it

Enough of planning; now it's time to get into action and execute. Don't wait for things to get perfect. The best way is to start and improvise as you progress. You have your schedule in place, begin performing tasks one at a time as per the pre-defined timelines. It might be difficult initially since forming new habits is never easy. However, keep your sights on the end goal and remind yourself why you are doing it? Why did you start on this journey? What are you going to get on the other side of it? If your why is aligned to your core values, you will overcome even the hardest resistances. As per studies, it can take anywhere from 18 days to 254 days to cultivate a new habit. However, in practical experience, it becomes a part of your routine if you can perform a new activity for 30 days. The message is clear, stick to the schedule for 30 days, come what may.

8.Review the Progress

Once you have started with your newly formed schedule and an action plan, it's essential to monitor and review the progress. It is a critical element in achieving the goal. It acts as a feedback mechanism. This helps identify what's working and what's not working for you. It also lets you the opportunity for timely course correction if things are not working out as planned. I recommend a weekly review to take stock.

9.Do the course correction if required

You may not like a workout schedule, or you may not want a specific diet plan. Or you may find that you are not getting the desired results from particular brain exercises. Instead of just continuing with the same stuff, it would make sense to try new techniques and tools to yield better results. The review process allows you to identify the steps where course correction is required. In this step, you go ahead, replace and reboot the process.

10.Persist & repeat

The final step in the blueprint is to persist and repeat the entire process till you have realized your Fortune. It depends entirely on your objective, whatever is the definition of fortune for you, material wealth, spiritual, emotional well-being, or something else. Whatever it is that you aspire to achieve, just go for it.

My Compliments to you for reading till the end. The fact that you are reading these final few lines is an indicator of your commitment to learning. I am sure you would have prepared your Focus to Fortune blueprint by now and would be raring to go.

I wish you all the success in your journey to **Master your Focus & Make a Fortune**.

****

Synopsis: Chapter 5

Integrate all the knowledge and information of previous sections to design the personalized blueprint for customized you. The blueprint comprises of below steps:

1.Know Yourself

The first step of the process is self-discovery. Knowing self provides clarity to questions like:

- What forms our core?
- What drives us?
- What motivates us?

Reduce distractions, set aside more time for yourself, and become more conscious of your inner self. Once you've done that, you'll better understand your foundation and the answers to the questions listed above.

2.Identify your Goal

Having a goal or an outcome provides clarity of purpose to progress in life. Self-awareness (Step 1) allows us to identify the core quality or value which defines us and is intrinsic to our personality. We must ensure that our outcome is aligned with it. Set your ultimate end goals, break them down into sub-goals with clear-cut timelines, and go about them one step at a time.

3.Train the Brain

A trained brain is better equipped to overcome obstructions and keep moving. At any point in time, we have several negative thoughts hovering in our minds, which stop us from taking action and make it difficult to persist in the face of adversity. Any combination of the techniques mentioned in the section, **“How to master the Focus,”** can be utilized to train the mind. Recap of mind training techniques :

1. Practicing Mindfulness
2. Practicing Meditation
3. Sleep
4. Brain Exercises

The application of mind training techniques allows better control, removes negative thoughts and negative emotions, and limits mind wandering to focus on our outcome single-mindedly.

4.Train the body

A healthy & fit body makes us feel energetic and much more committed. Any worthwhile goal requires considerable effort. To retain the focus for long hours and work consistently becomes more manageable if you are in the best of your health and vice-versa. As discussed in the earlier chapter, two essential elements of a healthy & disease-free life are:
1.Regular Exercise
2.Nutritious diet

Choose an exercise routine, which goes with your personality and lifestyle depending upon your age, weight, and nature of work. Make your personalized diet plan, taking into account your calorie requirement and medical conditions, if any.

5.Align the Environment

The next step requires cutting the distractions that interfere with you and don’t focus. Distractions can broadly be classified into two broad categories:

1.Physical environment
2.People

The physical environment comprises the workplace, infrastructure, noise, electronic gadgets, temperature, light, etc. People include your colleagues in the workplace. Use the relevant tips & techniques shared in," How **to Master the Focus"** section & apply them at your workplace to eliminate distractions from offline & online sources.

6.Define a Schedule

The schedule includes the tasks to be performed on a daily, weekly, fortnightly basis.
Exercising the mind & body via mindfulness, meditation, physical workout, diet, etc., are part of the daily routine. Once identified what needs to be done, the bottom line is to put all the activities in a schedule by calendarizing them day-wise and assigning time slots.

7.Just do it

You have your schedule in place, start performing tasks one at a time as per the pre-defined timelines. Stick to the plan for 30 days, come what may.

8.Review the Progress

Once you have started with your newly formed schedule and an action plan, it's essential to monitor and review the progress. It is a critical element in achieving the goal. I recommend a weekly review to take stock.

9.Do the course correction if required

The review process allows you to identify the steps where course correction is required. In this step, you go ahead, replace and reboot the process.

10.Persist & repeat

The final step in the blueprint is to persist and repeat the entire process till you have realized your Fortune. Whatever it is that you aspire to achieve, just go for it.

Synopsis: Full Book

Introduction

- **Focus** is a crucial element that helps us to concentrate on our task and accomplish it faster.

- **Clarity** of goals and single-minded focus enables people to be super successful despite not completing a formal education.

- **Focus** differentiates an ordinary person from the extraordinary one.

- **To reach** the final destination, you must cut through the distractions.

- **Mastering** the focus allows you to make a **Fortune**.

- **Four steps** to master the focus are knowing:

    - What is focus?

    - Why do we need to focus?

    - Why can't we focus?

    - How to focus?

- There are **two critical elements** of any transformation:

    1.Awareness: Knowing what you don't know.

    2.Action: Application of the knowledge.

Chapter 1: What is Focus?

- **Focus** is directed attention. It is the act of concentrating attention or effort on one single thing. We must ignore several other things to focus our attention and energy on one thing. It is the thinking skill that helps overcome procrastination, act, and continue the attention and effort until completing a task.

- **Doing One Thing At A Time (DOTAT)** is an essential principle of focus.

- **Warren Buffet's 5/25** rule of elimination is an excellent way to identify the priorities and decide what to focus on.
    - Make a list of 25 goals
    - Circle the top 5 goals
    - Write the top 5 goals in list A.
    - Write the remaining 20 in the list B.
    - Focus on achieving the goals in list A.
    - Move to list B, only once list A is complete

- The current era is known as the **Age of Distraction**. This is because there are so many things vying for our attention. Without mastering the art of focus, it's challenging to achieve anything meaningful without losing the plot.

- **Attention Residue** occurs during multi-tasking when we shift from one task to another without completing the first task. As a result, the second task only gets partial attention since some attention is still engaged in task one. This doesn't allow the focus and causes distraction.

Chapter 2
Why do we need to Focus?

- **Focus** a crucial element, the absence or presence of which has far-reaching effects in all the areas of our life. It can make us, and it can break us.

- **Mind** and **focus** have a strong connection. Therefore, focus on positive thoughts gets the favorable outcome and vice-versa.

- The critical importance of focus can be broadly classified into two segments:

  - **Achieving Excellence**: Individuals with high command of focus have excelled in their chosen area, which helped them create a fortune. To achieve success, focus is a must.

  - **Averting Disaster**: High focus tasks and jobs require excellent focus mastery and concentration. Loss of attention in such situations has disastrous repercussions.

- **No Focus** leads to **No Fortune**.

- **Top 10** benefits of focus.

  - ✓ Controlling the Mind
  - ✓ Improving the memory & concentration
  - ✓ Creative Imagination
  - ✓ More Clarity
  - ✓ Enhanced Self-Awareness

- ✓ Feeling of positivity
- ✓ Better Decision Making
- ✓ Better Problem-Solving Skills
- ✓ Minimizing errors
- ✓ High Efficiency

❖ To achieve the ultimate goal, we require **Long Term Focus (LTF).**

❖ To excel in daily tasks, we need to sharpen **Short Term Concentration. (STF)**

❖ **Long Term Focus (LTF)+Short Term Concentration (STF)=Success**

Chapter 3
Why is it difficult to Focus?

To understand why it is challenging to focus, we must understand the various elements impacting our concentration.
Broad classification of factors impacting focus:

❖ **Internal state factors:** Comprises of intrinsic elements and can be controlled at our end. These can be further subdivided into the state of mind(psychology) and state of the body(physiology).

- **Psychology of focus (State of Mind):** The guiding factors which determine the psychology of focus can be enumerated as under:

a) **Emotional states**: Positive as well as negative emotional states are included in this:

Negative emotional state: Low emotional state creates stress. Stress signaling weakens the prefrontal cortex, responsible for higher functions like critical thinking, impulse inhibition & the ability to focus. Fear, worry, anxiety are some causes of a negative emotional state.

Positive emotional state: High emotional state increases the adrenaline levels above permissible levels, making it difficult to concentrate. Fixation to sensory pleasures like tasty food, pleasant environment, and physical appearance causes a positive emotional state, making it challenging to focus.

Yerkes-Dodson Law: To have a good concentration, there has to be an optimum level of arousal. So, it essentially states that a balance between positive and negative emotional states is a must to focus and work efficiently.

b) Mind-wandering: The human mind wanders for approx.—50% of the time. While we may focus, the mind travels in the past and future instead of being present. The phenomenon is even more common for routine activities like walking and shopping that don't require extraordinary effort. As per the MRI scan studies, mind wandering happens even while we rest and do nothing. Various brain parts regulate this activity, and this phenomenon is known as the brain's default mode network.

Our brain is calibrated for arousal at the optimum level. If the activity is monotonous and boring, it starts looking for exciting alternatives for engagement by traveling to the past or future. Conversely, the brain looks for relief by searching the pleasurable activities in the mind stack if it is a highly complex task. The excessive wandering of the mind causes tension and digresses attention from critical tasks. It also translates to excessive errors and poor decision-making.

c)Skeptical doubt: Self-doubt is a state of indecisiveness of mind. It is an outcome of negative thoughts. Negative thoughts give birth to negative emotions like stress, worry, anxiety, fear, and doubt. Negative emotions distract the mind from being focused on the present & cause inaction.

d)Brain alertness: Attentiveness of the brain varies during the day depending on the biological clock. The concentration levels reach the maximum depending on the natural rhythm of the body. Sleep plays a vital role in determining brain alertness levels—consistent sleep deprivation for long-duration damages the brain cells resulting in reduced cognitive performance. Lack of brain alertness makes the simplest of tasks challenging.

f) Focus & neuro-science

Attention: It is the process by which the brain concentrates on the most critical information and ignores the rest. There are two types of attention:

1.Top-down attention or Endogenous attention: It's a process where the brain guides and decides the object of attention. The focus of attention is decided basis the priority of work to be accomplished. The neocortex part of the brain drives endogenous attention.

2.Bottom-up attention or Exogenous attention: Our senses drive it. The strongest of senses compels the brain to determine the object of focus. The primitive brain is responsible for this function. For example, while in a crowded marketplace, the loudest of noise, strongest of smell, or the outlet's aesthetics attracts our attention.

Classification of attention, basis ability to concentrate:

1.**Selective attention**: Focused attention for a short period while ignoring distractions.
2.**Multi-tasking**: Shifting attention between multiple tasks.
3.**Sustained attention**: Selective attention for an extended duration.

Neuro Chemistry of attention

Neuromodulators that aid attention and focus are as under:

Acetylcholine (Ach): It helps in paying attention, learning, and memory retention.

Dopamine: It determines what to focus on based on past information. It provides the flexibility of focus by scanning the records.

Norepinephrine: This neurotransmitter is responsible for brain alertness. It stimulates brain arousal and restricts cells that promote sleep. Enhanced brain alertness alleviates cognitive functioning, focus, and reaction times.

Noradrenaline: Planning an execution is governed by this neurotransmitter.

- **Physiology of focus (State of Body)**: It covers the body's general well-being and its impact on focus.

Chronic health conditions responsible for poor focus and concentration can be summarized as under:

a) Alcohol use disorder: Excessive intake of alcohol causes chemical changes in the brain. The alterations give you a feeling of pleasure while consuming alcohol. If you stop drinking, you experience withdrawal symptoms, leading to the disorientation of the brain, lack of concentration and focus.

b) Attention deficit hyperactivity disorder (ADHD): It's a mental health condition that causes hyperactivity and impulsivity. Sitting in one place and concentration on one task becomes difficult under this condition.

There are three types of ADHD

#Predominantly inattentive: Trouble in focusing, following instructions, and finishing work.
#Predominantly hyperactive: Fidgeting, interrupting people during conversation.
#Combined: Most common type, which is a combination of the above two conditions.

c)Chronic fatigue syndrome: Extreme weariness and exhaustion of the body, which can't be cured by rest and is not the result of any medical condition. It causes insomnia, memory loss, reduced brain alertness, and diminished concentration.

d)Concussion: It is also known as mild traumatic injury. An injury that causes the head and brain to shake back and forth rapidly causes a concussion. Accidents like car collisions, falling from a height may result in trauma. Memory problems, dizziness, blurred vision, headache, slow reaction, etc., are the effects.

e)Dementia: Loss of cognitive function signifies dementia. It is caused by the degeneration of neurons in the brain or changes in other body systems that impair the functioning of neurons. It impacts memory, thinking, behavior, judgment, frequent mood changes, difficulty in completing daily tasks.

f) Epilepsy: It causes seizures, which are sudden bursts of electrical activity in the brain. High fever, very low blood sugar, alcohol withdrawal symptom, etc., are the possible causes. Loss of consciousness and disorientation are the possible outcomes.

g) Insomnia: It is the condition of sleep deprivation for long durations.

Acute or short-term insomnia: Stress, traumatic events, changes in sleeping habits, sleeping place. Certain medical conditions, jet lag, etc.

Chronic Insomnia: Lasts for three months and above. Causes include medical conditions like arthritis or back pain, psychological issues-anxiety or depression, substance abuse, diabetes, etc.
Outcomes: Fatigue, not feeling fresh, reduced brain alertness, lack of concentration.

h) Depression: Feeling of sadness and upset for extended duration classifies depression. Causes include loss of interest, anxiety, sadness, hopelessness, pessimism, anger, irritation, restlessness, etc.
Outcomes: Reduced energy, chronic fatigue, lack of concentration, poor decision making, memory loss, etc.

i)Anxiety: It can happen to anyone for any reason, such as before a big event or an important decision. However, anxiety for a prolonged duration causes restlessness, fear, panic, dread, and irritability.

- **External state Factors:** The broad categorization of external factors can be done as under:

  - **Aesthetics:** Good and organized ambiance aids focus, while a bad one makes us anxious.
  - **Sensory:** Type of lighting, temperature, sound, smell, color decide the comfort level, relaxed state, or anxiety.
  - **People:** Progressive and like-minded people sharing similar objective aid focus. Chatty co-workers and non-aligned people in the surroundings cause distraction.
  - **Culture & values**: Conflicting behaviors and non-aligned culture creates a toxic environment. In addition, negative emotions like stress, anxiety, and worry limit the ability to focus.
  - **Familiarity**: The absence of known surroundings leads to a lack of clarity. Uncertainty breeds anxiousness, worry, stress and reduces concentration.

Understanding Distraction: A thing that prevents from giving full attention to something else. Hunger, exhaustion, illness, stress, etc., are internal distractions. Social interactions, music, text messages, phone calls, etc., are all external distractions.

The top 12 External distractions at the workplace are as under:

1.Office colleagues: Regular interruptions adversely impact the concentration disrupt the flow of work.

2.Noisy work environment: High noise levels cause distraction from the task at hand.

3.Emails: Receiving email notifications and checking them simultaneously while working on an important project distracts and delays the pace of work.

4.Mobile Phone: Frequently checking the mobile phone during the day diverts attention, interrupts workflow, and causes brain fatigue.

5.Social media: A glaring example of technology ruling brains. Likes, comments, and views aid the dopamine rush leading to high adrenaline. Conversely, lack of engagement causes low self-esteem, stress, worry. Either way, it causes a lack of concentration.

6.Meetings: Excess of meetings breaks the rhythm, reduces concentration.

7.Multi-tasking: It causes strain, making it difficult to concentrate and focus.

8.Messy workplace: Mess at work diverts attention from the creation to surroundings. This acts as a persistent reminder of all that needs to be done.

9.Excessive supervision: Micromanaging things is a dual-edged sword. On the one hand, you lose your precious time interfering in someone else's work. While on the other, too much control makes the other person conscious and distracts from performing the task efficiently.

10.Comfort: Too much or too little comfort reduces the brain's alertness. Relaxing position reduces brain alertness by inducing sleep. An extremely uncomfortable posture may cause pain and stray the attention from work.
11.Lighting: Dim lights cause strain on the eyes, reducing concentration. High rays may cause headaches.

12.Temperature: Warm temperature induces sleep, and cold temperature causes uneasiness. Extreme weather conditions are known to make focusing an arduous task.

Chapter 4: How to Master the Focus?

Focus is essentially a muscle. So, if you're wondering how to focus better, it's a skill that must be practiced regularly. That means you'll have to work hard to avoid checking your phone every two minutes if you want to finish that project. Most people can't concentrate for two reasons:

1.We are never taught how to concentrate.
2.We don't practice concentration.

To become a focus expert, it's essential to understand the mind. Once we know it, we can control it. Once we can manage it, we can master the focus.
There are two critical things to learn concentration:

- Awareness
- Mind

Consider awareness as the glowing ball of light and mind as the vast field with various chambers. Each chamber is occupied by emotions like anger, jealousy, hunger, greed, sex, joy, happiness, etc. The glowing ball of self-awareness can travel to any area of mind and illuminate it. Whichever room it lights up, we become conscious of it, and the awareness goes up.

Concentration requires keeping the awareness of one particular area for an extended period.

How to practice concentration?

One of the best ways is to allow awareness to remain on one thing for a long duration. So, keep looking for such opportunities throughout the day. For example, while talking to your spouse, partner, friend, or family member, imagine keeping the ball of awareness on them and giving them undivided attention. That's the best way to practice.

To focus on the present, it's imperative to get rid of these worries about the future and calm yourself. Focus is choosing the proper thought among thousands of ideas going in our minds. To do so, a few simple steps may help:

1.Learn to distinguish between disturbing and non-disturbing thoughts. One non-disturbing thought can knock off all the troubling thoughts and bring you back to focus.

2.Constantly being worried about the goal or what we want to achieve shifts focus to the future and drifts us away from the present. Unless we work on what we are good at and remain focused on the present, it's impossible to achieve the future goal.

3. Replace To do list with Not-To-Do List. This implies preparing a list of all the stuff, which you are not supposed to do.

Mastering the focus requires control of self and managing the external environment. Therefore, we will be covering the how part of the focus in three segments:

- How to train the mind?
- How to train the body?
- How to manage the environment?

How to train the mind?

Essential methods & techniques that can be used to train the mind to focus better are:
1.Mindfulness
2.Meditation
3.Sleep
4.Exercising the brain

1.Mindfulness: The ability to be fully present, aware of where we are and what we're doing, and not unduly reactive or overwhelmed by what's going on around us is known as mindfulness.

Key Benefits Of Mindfulness

- ✓ Memory Enhancement
- ✓ Meta-cognitive Awareness
- ✓ Reduced Anxiety
- ✓ Low Emotional Reactivity
- ✓ Visual Attention Processing
- ✓ Stress Reduction
- ✓ Reduction in Physical Pain

Group-based Mindfulness Techniques

- **Mindfulness-Based Stress Reduction (MBSR):** It is a group technique that emphasizes yoga, meditation, and other similar activities.

- **Mindfulness-Based Cognitive Therapy (MBCT):** Mindful breathing and meditation are used in MBCT.It focuses on teaching techniques to reframe feelings and not eradicating them.

Common mindfulness techniques

- **Focussed attention on the breath**: It cultivates present mindedness by focussing on the breath movement.

- **Open awareness**: It promotes staying focused on the present moment by being aware of the surroundings. Paying attention to the objects in your vicinity and sensation from the various elements can help to relax and cleanse the mind.

Illustrations for practicing mindfulness in daily activities:

a) Walking: Notice the rhythm of each step, feel the breeze, listen to noises, savor the colors. Attention to all these elements helps to focus on the present.

b) Interactions: During conversations, listen with an open mind. Avoid being judgemental in arguments. Refrain from digging out the past instances; concentrate on the current situation only.

c) Public appearances: To reduce the stress before a public appearance, reflect on the feelings. Accept the feelings and remind yourself that these are momentary emotions and do not necessarily define you. Feel the muscles as they relax.

Mindfulness Tips:

1.Mindful Breathing
2.Engagement in the Task
3.Savour the process
4.Do Nothing
5.Rewind
6.Be mindful of the cognitive process
7.Sef-consciousness
8.Heightened awareness
9.Immersion in nature
10.Observe the drift

2.Meditation: It is a series of techniques designed to promote heightened awareness and focused concentration. It offers numerous psychological advantages and can also be used as a form of psychotherapy.

Concepts for practicing meditation:

1.Choose a peaceful place
2.Choose a short duration session of 5 to or 10 min, to begin with
3.Choose a comfortable body posture
4.Focus on your breath and pay attention to each sensation while breathing
5.Notice your thoughts, and whenever the mind wanders, concentrate on your breath

Forms of Meditation

1.Concentrative meditation: Requires to focus on a single item while phasing out everything else. Choose what to focus on-breath, word, or a mantra.

Steps involved

1. Choose the Target
2. Choose a position
3. Get into a relaxed state
4. Pay attention to the target
5. Stop self-talk
6. Eliminate the fear of failure

2.Mindfulness meditation: It relaxes the mind and body by slowing down the speed of thoughts. It involves deep breathing and awareness of the body and mind.
Mindfulness-based stress reduction and mindfulness-based cognitive therapy are examples of mindfulness meditation.

Being aware and active in the present moment and self-acceptance are the main objectives.

Steps involved

1. Choose a comfortable position
2. Set a timer
3. Notice your breathing
4. Notice your thoughts
5. Take a break

Tips for practicing mindfulness meditation in daily routine:

- ✓ Brushing the teeth
- ✓ Dishwashing
- ✓ Washing clothes
- ✓ Driving
- ✓ Working out
- ✓ Getting kids to sleep

How meditation improves focus?

It improves brain structure by rewiring neural circuits. As a result, most-used connections are strengthened, and the least used ones are weeded off.

Meditation improves the volume of the brain region, which is crucial for memory & information retention. Regular meditation also reduces the size of the amygdala, a brain area involved in processing negative emotions like fear.

3.Sleep: Sleep permits the brain and body to settle down and engage in healing processes, which helps in the improvement of physical and mental performance. Lack of sleep disrupts the essential functions which affect thinking, concentration, energy levels, and mood.

According to brain plasticity theory, sleep permits neurons to restructure. As a result, it helps in clearing harmful by-products from the brain.

Key benefits of sleep:

- ✓ Improved brain efficiency
- ✓ The clarity to comprehend information
- ✓ Memory retention
- ✓ Alleviates Creativity
- ✓ Flushing out toxins from the brain

4.Brain exercises to strengthen focus: Focus is like a muscle. Exercising the brain regularly is essential for sustained concentration and focus. Brain exercises to sharpen the focus:

- ✓ Solve puzzles
- ✓ Card Games
- ✓ Building Vocabulary
- ✓ Leveraging senses
- ✓ Learn a skill
- ✓ Teach a skill
- ✓ Play or listen to music
- ✓ Explore variety in the routine
- ✓ Learn a new language
- ✓ Concentrate on others

How to train the body to focus?

The two main elements which play a vital role in preparing the body and improving concentration are:

1.Exercise

2.Nutrition

1.Exercise: Regular workout makes you feel more energetic, ensures better sleep, creates better memories, generates positive emotions, and relaxes your brain.

Crucial benefits of regular exercise:

- ✓ Enhanced energy
- ✓ Enhanced mood
- ✓ Defends against illnesses
- ✓ Improved memory, cognition, and learning

It also helps as an effective cure against mental health conditions:

- ➢ **Depression**: Physical activity causes the brain to release endorphins, which make you feel happy. It also helps in diverting attention and breaking the loop of negative thoughts.
- ➢ **Anxiety**: The release of endorphins relieves tension and stress and improves overall well-being.
- ➢ **Stress**: Exercise helps relax the muscles by releasing tension in the body and producing endorphins in the brain.
- ➢ **ADHD**: Raise in neurotransmitters like dopamine, norepinephrine, and serotonin levels while exercising aids in focus and attention.
- ➢ **Trauma**: Focussing on the body while exercising frees the nervous system and eliminates immobility stress associated with trauma. Cross-movement exercises that work both arms and legs work the best.

Tips for beginning with physical activity:

- ✓ Start small
- ✓ Workout in a high energy state
- ✓ Concentrate

- ✓ Be at ease
- ✓ Reward yourself
- ✓ Work out in groups

How to train the body without going to the gym?

- ✓ Doing household chores
- ✓ Workout on the go
- ✓ Fun with the family
- ✓ Use your imagination

2.Nutrition: Food provides raw resources required for the correct functioning of the nervous system, mind, and body. The Digestive system and brain have a complex relationship. Nutrition is vital to provide the nourishment required for the healthy functioning of the body and mind.

- Macronutrients are also known as big nutrients. These include protein, fats, and carbohydrates. Balanced meals comprising 50% carbs,30% fats, and 20% protein are good to go.

- Micronutrients are the vitamins and minerals found in our meals. B Vitamins, Vitamin D, and magnesium are the micronutrients essential for focus.

In addition to macro and micronutrients, there are some other elements impacting focus and productivity.

Antioxidants: These are the plant chemicals, which prevent the accumulation of dangerous free radicals. Free radicals cause inflammation and may damage brain cells.

Gut-brain axis: it is the line of communication between the brain and digestive system. It is the bidirectional connection that happens between the gut and central nervous system. The healthy and harmful bacteria ratio determines the positive or negative impact on the brain and central nervous system. Unhealthy balance causes brain fog, fatigue, loss of focus, and productivity.

Essentials for a healthy gut:

- ✓ Probiotics and fermented foods: Fermented foods like yogurt provide healthy bacteria, which helps in keeping digestive problems at bay.
- ✓ Eating a low inflammation diet: Inflammation is associated with brain illness disease like Alzheimer's. Foods like fatty fish, chia seeds, flax seeds are rich in anti-inflammatory omega-3 fats, which counter the free radical activity and control inflammation.
- ✓ High fiber consumption: Fiber is pre-biotic; it feeds the good bacteria in the stomach. Fruits, vegetables, nuts, seeds, beans are all high in fiber.
- ✓ Consume good fats: It helps in healthy brain functioning.

Superfoods to boost focus and concentration

a) Water: It is required for all brain functions because it provides essential electrical energy. Lack of water in the brain can result in:

- Difficulty in focusing and paying attention
- Brain exhaustion
- Fog in the head
- Aches and pains
- Sleep disruptions
- Irritableness

Recommended water intake is 13 cups for men and 9 cups for women.

b) Blueberries: It improves concentration and memory by increasing oxygen and blood flow to the brain. In addition, it is rich in antioxidants, vitamin c, vitamin E, and flavonoids.

c)Avocados: These are rich in healthy fats and other essential nutrients that boost brain function. In addition, avocados have high protein content and the lowest sugar content.

d)Leafy Greens: These are rich in potassium which speeds up the connections between neurons, making them more responsive. Lutein is also abundant in green plants such as spinach and kale. It improves learning, memory and preserves brain function.

e) Coffee: Caffeine and antioxidants, the two main components of coffee, cause increased alertness, improve mood and sharpen concentration.

f) Turmeric: Curcumin is the critical element in turmeric, passing the blood-brain barrier and benefiting brain cells.

g) Broccoli: It is high in antioxidants, vitamin k, and other vital plant components beneficial for enhanced memory functions.

h) Pumpkin Seeds: These are high in antioxidants, which protect the body and brain from the effects of free radicals. Magnesium, iron, zinc, and copper are the other brain health minerals found in abundant quantities.

i)Dark Chocolate: Contains flavonoids that help in learning and memory functions.

j) Nuts: These are rich in healthy fats, antioxidants, and vitamin E required for healthy heart function and boost memory.

k) Oranges: One medium-size orange can suffice the vitamin C requirement for a whole day. Vitamin C is critical for maintaining mental health.

l)Eggs: Eggs are rich in vitamins B6 and B12, which are vital for healthy brain function.

m)Green Tea: The presence of caffeine boosts alertness, performance, memory, and focus.

n) Fatty Fish: Salmon, trout, and sardines are examples of fatty fish. These are rich in omega-3 fatty acids, which are required for the smooth functioning of the brain.

How to manage the external environment?

The external environment includes the physical environment we live in and the people we are surrounded with. The prominent sources of distraction and the effective ways of dealing with external environmental factors can be summarized as under:

1)Chatty colleagues: Have a one-to-one discussion with the concerned person to express your concern or close the door when engaged in deep work.

2)Noisy workplace: Cut the noise by either closing the door, shifting your workplace, putting on the headphones, or working from home.

3)Email interruptions: Effective ways of tackling it include:

- ✓ Blocking off time to check mails
- ✓ Offline method of operation
- ✓ Interval checking

- ✓ Avoid starting the day with emails.

4)Smartphone: Put your phone out of your reach so that you can concentrate on your task and do away with the temptation of checking it every few minutes.

5)Social media: Set specified timelines for checking social media. Turn off all notifications to avoid being distracted.

6)Meetings: Ten ways to avoid wasting time and conducting productive meetings:

- ✓ Set a positive tone for each meeting
- ✓ Appoint a clear leader to drive the agenda
- ✓ Only the required participants should be present for the meeting
- ✓ Define clear action steps at the end
- ✓ Make the meeting's agenda crystal clear
- ✓ Ensure that meetings are of optimum length only
- ✓ Begin and end in time
- ✓ Align the environment

7)Multi-Tasking: Using time blocks to focus on one task at a time helps to overcome it.60-60-30 method of time blocking and Pomodoro technique can be used to overcome it.

8)Micro-management: Tips to get rid of micro-management:

- ✓ Delegation
- ✓ Establish clear goals
- ✓ Quit perfection
- ✓ Employ the correct personnel
- ✓ Ask employee preference for supervision

9)Cluttered Work Place: A chaotic work environment resembles a disorganized mind and obstructs focus.

Removing unwanted clutter and mess creates a positive work environment, making it easier to focus.

10)Lighting: Certain sorts of lights elicit particular responses, such as the urge to sleep, relax, or be stimulated. The right kind of lighting boosts the mood, enhances energy and alertness.

11)Temperature: Temperature affects pupil attention span. The ideal climate, which aids concentration and focussing ability, is between 70-78 degrees.

Chapter 5
Focus To Fortune Blueprint

Integrate all the knowledge and information of previous sections to design the personalized blueprint for customized you. The blueprint comprises of below steps:

1.Know Yourself

The first step of the process is self-discovery. Knowing self provides clarity to questions like:

- What forms our core?
- What drives us?
- What motivates us?

Reduce distractions, set aside more time for yourself, and become more conscious of your inner self. Once you've done that, you'll better understand your foundation and the answers to the questions listed above.

2.Identify your Goal

Having a goal or an outcome provides clarity of purpose to progress in life.

Self-awareness (Step 1) allows us to identify the core quality or value which defines us and is intrinsic to our personality. We must ensure that our outcome is aligned with it.

Set your ultimate end goals, break them down into sub-goals with clear-cut timelines, and go about them one step at a time.

3.Train the Brain

A trained brain is better equipped to overcome obstructions and keep moving. At any point in time, we have several negative thoughts hovering in our minds, which stop us from taking action and make it difficult to persist in the face of adversity.

Any combination of the techniques mentioned in the section, **"How to master the Focus,"** can be utilized to train the mind. Recap of mind training techniques :

I. Practicing Mindfulness
II. Practicing Meditation
III. Sleep
IV. Brain Exercises

The application of mind training techniques allows better control, removes negative thoughts and negative emotions, and limits mind wandering to focus on our outcome single-mindedly.

4.Train the body

A healthy & fit body makes us feel energetic and much more committed. Any worthwhile goal requires considerable effort. To retain the focus for long hours and work consistently becomes more manageable if you are in the best of your health and vice-versa. As discussed in the earlier chapter, two essential elements of a healthy & disease-free life are:

1.Regular Exercise
2.Nutritious diet

Choose an exercise routine, which goes with your personality and lifestyle depending upon your age, weight, and nature of work. Make your personalized diet plan, taking into account your calorie requirement and medical conditions, if any.

5.Align the Environment

The next step requires cutting the distractions that interfere with you and don't focus.
Distractions can broadly be classified into two broad categories:

1.Physical environment
2.People

The physical environment comprises the workplace, infrastructure, noise, electronic gadgets, temperature, light, etc. People include your colleagues in the workplace.

Use the relevant tips & techniques shared in," How **to Master the Focus"** section & apply them at your workplace to eliminate distractions from offline & online sources.

6.Define a Schedule

The schedule includes the tasks to be performed on a daily, weekly, fortnightly basis.
Exercising the mind & body via mindfulness, meditation, physical workout, diet, etc., are part of the daily routine.
Once identified what needs to be done, the bottom line is to put all the activities in a schedule by calendarizing them day-wise and assigning time slots.

7.Just do it

You have your schedule in place, start performing tasks one at a time as per the pre-defined timelines.
Stick to the schedule for 30 days, come what may.

8.Review the Progress

Once you have started with your newly formed schedule and an action plan, it's essential to monitor and review the progress. It is a critical element in achieving the goal.
I recommend a weekly review to take stock.

9.Do the course correction if required

The review process allows you to identify the steps where course correction is required. In this step, you go ahead, replace and reboot the process.

10.Persist & repeat

The final step in the blueprint is to persist and repeat the entire process till you have realized your Fortune.

Whatever it is that you aspire to achieve, just go for it.

Bonus Hacks to Master The Focus

"When things get blurry, it's time to adjust the FOCUS"

-Lalit Hundalani

Hack 1:The FOCUS Rule

Sam Horn, a communications consultant and author of several books, offers a clever hack to improve focus, using the FOCUS acronym:

F is for Five More: Whenever you find work tedious or difficult and feel like quitting, just do five more. What that five means specifically depends on the task at hand. It could be five more minutes of running, five more pages of reading, or five more minutes of cleaning. The idea is to get over the momentary obstruction, which is enticing you to give up. The chances are that once you do five more, you will get the focus back on track to carry on.

O is for One thing at a Time: What to do when you are engaged in a task, and suddenly a stray thought crosses your mind, reminding you of another incomplete job. For example, as I sat to write this piece, I recalled the video to be edited, mail to be sent to the client, and the upcoming coaching session in the evening. To avoid being distracted, I wrote these things in my notebook and continued with what I was doing. This allows me to keep distractions at bay, and making notes of the actionable also reminds me to attend to them later.

C is for Conquer Procrastination. Next time when you feel like putting off a task for later, just ask yourself:

Why do I need to do this?

What are the consequences of not doing it?

How will delaying add any value?

These questions will get you the required clarity and provide the required push for taking inspired action.

U is for Use Pavlovian Rituals. A little warm-up reminds and sends a signal to the brain for the work to be done. For example, doctors scrub up before surgery; musicians play scales; tennis players bounce a ball three times before serving & cricketers take a stance at the batting crease. The rituals send a signal to the brain: "Game On!".Choose a pattern commensurate with your work and help train your brain to switch into focus mode on command.

S is for Set Specific Start and End Times. Give your brain-specific and clear instructions for the start and end timings. You may not always get the job done in the allotted time, but the use of clear instructions helps you focus and boost your productivity.

Hack 2:The Lazy Genius way

According to Chris Bailey, best-selling author of the book Hyperfocus, our attention is focused or unfocused. Although focused attention gets all the work done, unfocussed attention is also equally powerful. Focused attention makes us productive, while unfocussed attention makes us creative. Ideas strike in moments when we are not concentrating on any particular thing. It could be in a shower, walking, reading, or doing nothing. It happens due to the brain's phenomenon of mind wandering. As per studies, 48% of the time mind wanders in the future, 28% in the present, and 12% in the past, and the remaining is blank. Three critical things happen when we are just lazing around and doing nothing:

Rest. While at rest, we don't direct our attention. This is known as the state of conscious mind-wandering or "scatter focus." Our brain is calibrated for arousal at the optimum level. If the activity is monotonous and boring, it starts looking for exciting alternatives for engagement by traveling to the past or future. It starts craving novelty and pleasure, which leads to the generation of new ideas.

Plan. During the scattered phase of attention, we think 14 times more about the future. We contemplate long-term goals seven times as frequently during rest mode(provided we have goals). So strategic laziness acts as a ready reckoner for long-term goals and pushes into action.

Discover ideas. Mind-wandering while doing nothing connects all three mental destinations: the past, the present, and the future. This helps in connecting the dots and get creative insights. For example, you may recall an idea you read a few weeks back and combine it to solve a current work situation.

When we're idle, it doesn't look like we're doing much. But mentally, the exact opposite is true. That's what makes you the lazy genius.

Hack3

Conscious Procrastination

This hack essentially requires you to sleep over the problem if you can't find the immediate solution. This technique uses the phenomenon of the Zeigarnik effect. According to this theory, incomplete tasks and pending decisions weigh more heavily on our minds than ones we've

finished—focus comes when we close these distracting open loops. As rightly mentioned by Chris Bailey, the Zeigarnik effect can do something stunning when we scatter our attention and let our minds wander. When we are stuck with an unresolved problem, it is stored in the front of our minds.

As a consequence, we connect each new experience to resolve this problem. Thus, while consciously we may not be working on the issue, we subconsciously do—the persistence results in finding the answer to the question while not being actively focused on it. There have been several examples of this effect where people arrived at solutions after being spurred by an external cue:

- ✓ Archimedes figured out how to calculate the volume of an irregular object when he noticed his bathwater overflowing.
- ✓ Newton came up with his theory of gravity when he saw an apple fall from a tree.
- ✓ The renowned physicist and Nobel laureate Richard Feynman took this a notch higher by consciously practicing scatter focus this routine. He would frequently visit the bars, where he could "watch the entertainment," and, when inspiration struck, scribble equations on cocktail napkins."

Hack 4:The 4 P method

The first P is Perform: When you are going to begin a task or project, just remind yourself that you need to perform your best. This creates a strong "why" for the brain to avoid distraction.

The second P is Process: It requires you to be engaged in the process and deliver high-quality work without worrying about the outcome.

The third P is Present: Which means focusing on the now rather than on what has happened in the past or what might happen in the future.

Finally, the fourth P is Productivity: Which requires identifying what needs to be done and eliminating the rest.

The method lets you accomplish better quality work, more success, and achievement of professional goals.

Hack 5:The 5 D method

The First D is Delete Distraction: With so many distractions abound, it's tough to focus. Setting the proper environment is helpful, which lets you work in distraction-free mode. Putting on noise-canceling headphones, storing the phone in a drawer or another room, and closing the door are some of the tactics that help create the right environment.

The second D is for Daily intention: List down the three things you want to accomplish. This shifts your focus and sets the intention on what's important. Prioritizing these things ensures that these tasks stand out from a laundry list of other, less important things.

The third D is for Difficult work: A per Parkinson's law, work tends to expand to fill the available time. Any spare time remaining is usually filled with distractions. Sometimes, distractions happen because we're not being challenged enough by our work, which means it is boring or too simple, letting the mind wander and looking for more exciting options. Assess your worklist on these parameters and take on more challenging projects. This will ensure that attention remains on the work at hand and time is utilized productively.

The fourth D is for Do more: This requires doing more challenging work to have no time for distractions. Stacking one difficult task after another leaves little room for less critical activities. So, do more heavy lifting.

The fifth D is for Deadline: This requires gamification of the process. Creating the timeline for completion of work helps in reverse-engineering the entire process. The brain starts working backward in a way that leads to timely completion of the task, leaving you with surplus time to fit in more.

Hack 6:The ICECREAM hack

Intensely focussed reading is one of the most effective brain exercises to boost concentration. Most of the time, when we read, attention wavers. This trick helps to overcome this phenomenon:

I is for Intense Focus: Commit to an intense, severe focus on reading for the defined time frame.5min- 10min is an excellent timeline, to begin with.

C is for Cutting the Crap: Set the distraction-free environment by eliminating all the elements, which might not contribute to the activity.

E is for Elimination: Eliminate any random thoughts that aim to stray your attention outside the book.

C is for Conscious: When you find yourself thinking about not being focused, make a conscious effort to change the script. Accept that these thoughts don't define you; neither is this your active thinking process.

R is for Reading: Continue reading irrespective of whatever is happening in your mind. Keep pulling your attention back on the page and the words until you have read at least a full page.

E is for Every day: Repeat the process every day. You can increase the time duration as you get better.

A is for Acknowledge: It is imperative to acknowledge yourself each time you complete the process. The sense of achievement makes you feel good and motivates you to repeat the process.

M is for Master: I am confident that repeating the process every day will undoubtedly make you an expert. So make it a habit till you master it.

Hack 7: 6M Management

Managing the 6 M of your schedule improves the focus and gets you started with what's important.

First M is for the Main task. Identify the single most crucial thing which is very important for you to accomplish on a specific day. Anchor your schedule around that task, which is non-negotiable. Explore other items in a to-do list; once you get over the main task.

The second M is for Managing energy. Ascertain the task, which would require maximum concentration and effort. Assign the heavy lifting task to the time of the day when you have full power. It will serve two advantages-one you will be able to do it faster, and the second, once you have done the most challenging work, completing the rest might seem like a breeze.

The third M is your Mailbox. Assign the timeframe for checking your mails and shut it on other times. Real-time response to mails is not required in the majority of circumstances. Two to three slots during the day are enough to take care of the mail menace.

The fourth M is for Mobile. Keep your mobile phone away from you while working. This is vital to control the urge of checking it every few minutes and delaying the work completion. Switch it off or put it in airplane mode for short durations of intense work. It contributes towards high-quality work.

Fifth M is for Mode. If you are working on a laptop or PC, try working on full-screen mode. This is a very effective way of keeping the attention only on the application you are working on. For example, reading an article in full-screen mode does away with toolbars at the top and bottom, the time clock, temperature, date, etc.

Sixth M is for the Morning. Mornings are very crucial and decide the fate of the remaining day. So how you utilize morning hours matters the most? Setting up a morning routine or morning ritual helps set the tone and gives the much-needed clarity for the work to be accomplished during the day.

Hack 8: Do the 5S.

5 S process helps in improving focus by making things simple and providing clarity:

Sort: I am sure you would have several things to accomplish, and where to start would be the challenge. Do a sorting of all that needs to be done and create a sequence basis the urgency and importance. Once you have arranged the activities in order, make a list. This gives the much-needed clarity on order to be followed for attending to priorities.

Single: From the list prepared in step 1, pick one task at the top of the order. Focus your attention on the completion of single activity at a time. Don't even think of attending to the next item till the first is done.

Simplify: Most of the time, we lose concentration due to the nature of the work, especially if it's a complex task. Breaking it down into small pieces and attending to one chunk at a time makes it simpler. So, simplify the process to make it easy, engaging, and enjoyable.

Silence: Fix the environment and workplace by eliminating unwanted noise which may interfere with your work. Too much noise creates overstimulation of the brain, not the ideal scenario for deep work. Silence helps in relaxing the mind, which aids in delivering high-quality output in less time.

Stick: Once you have decided on a specific activity or schedule, stick to it till completion. Frequent changes create confusion, and the flow is lost.

Hack 9: The ICSE framework

One of the key reasons for our inability to focus lies in our lack of self-belief. Self-doubt stimulates the brain, conceives negative emotions, and causes distraction. It's like losing the battle even more going for one.

The ICSE framework is targeted at strengthening the belief system by changing the brain codes.

I is for Identify: Specify which areas of your wheel of life you want the reprogramming to be done. Consider broad areas like health, career, wealth, family, relationship, personal growth, fun, and physical environment. Identify the areas where you are not content and want to work on.

C is for Codes: Once you have identified the relevant areas in step one, figure out the negative thoughts or codes you might carry in your head. Replace the harmful codes with positive ones. For example, I am not good at reading can be changed to I am a voracious reader. Get the power codes for all required areas where reprogramming needs to be done. Write down your personalized power codes which make you internally strong, and re-code your brain.

S is for Score: Give a score to yourself on a scale of 1 to 10 basis the current progress in the areas so identified in step 1. Also, write down the scores your want to achieve. For example, if the health is not good, the current rating would be three or four, and the projected score would be around 8 or 9. The scoring would give you clarity of the important reason for proceeding with this activity.

E is for Execute: Once you have completed the first three steps, it's time to execute. Start practicing your power codes daily. Do it even if you don't believe in them. Once you do daily affirmations, they will gradually seep into your subconscious mind and change your self-talk.
This framework is compelling. If done in the right way, it will code you to success like no other hack.

Hack 10: Focused Meditation

It's indeed a proven way to sharpen concentration skills in 5 simple steps. The good thing is that these sessions are short and can be practiced anywhere, anytime. So whether it's your home, office, or any other place, you can conveniently practice this technique. The only prerequisite is quiet surroundings.

Step 1:Identify a target to fix the focus. To begin with, you can choose your breath to focus on. It helps by shifting the focus internally and also does away with the requirement of any external prop.

Step 2:Get into a comfortable posture. If you sit on a chair, sit on the edge, relax your pelvic bones and place the feet firmly placed on the floor. If you are sitting on the floor, then sit straight so that your spine remains tall.

Step 3:Transition into a relaxed state. Loosen your shoulders and breathe from your belly. Repeat the process till you achieve a comfortable position.

Step 4:Turn your attention on the chosen target. Feel the sensations of sound, smell, touch, sight of your chosen focal point. If you have selected breathe as the focused target, then observe the feelings of exhaling and inhale as you continue with the process.

Step 5: Get rid of the fear of failure. If you find yourself unable to hold attention to the chosen target, don't worry. Compliment yourself on noticing the phenomenon and quietly bring yourself back to the present scenario. Repeat the process, and slowly you will get better at it. You can start with short sessions of 5min to 10 min and then build them up as you get better.

We can't help that our minds crave distraction. But what we can do is set ourselves up for success by adopting strategies to block distractions ahead of time, work with greater intention, and reclaim our attention, once and for all.

Trust, you will find these hacks helpful towards the objective of mastering your focus.

"Transformation requires you to Focus on who you want to be, not on who you already are"

Gratitude

Dear Reader

Pls, accept my heartfelt compliments and sincere gratitude for taking out your precious time to read this book. I hope you would have found the content to be useful for you. I expect that you are going to apply the learnings, knowledge & techniques to transform your life.

Feedback is very critical for continuous improvement and getting better at things. For an author, reviews constitute an integral part of the feedback mechanism. It encourages and pushes to perform better. I, therefore, look forward to an **honest review** from your end on www.Amazon.com

It will just take **60 seconds** for you but will mean a lot to me. It will help me reach out to more readers and work on your suggestions in the next book.

Thanks for your support and patience. I am looking forward to your review on www.Amazon.com.

Thanks

Lalit Hundalani

About the Author

Lalit Hundalani is India's leading **Peak Performance** & **Life transformation coach, Facilitator, Productivity Geek, Global Best Selling Author, Keynote Speaker & Mentor**. He is on a mission to empower 1 Million individuals to transform their lives.

Lalit is a certified leadership & strategic management professional from the prestigious **Indian Institute of Management Lucknow (IIML)**. He carries a rich experience of working with corporate sector catering to large & reputed organizations.

A lifelong learner, he is always eager to re-invent himself & keep exploring new paradigms. A follower and practitioner of the maxim of learn, do & teach, he ensures to practice and implement the concepts before preaching to others. He is firmly convinced about the enormity of human potential, which enables the change beyond imagination. The process of change begins with us & therefore fixing the inner-self holds the key to change in the outside world.

He is an avid blogger, You tuber, and fitness enthusiast. To connect and know more about him, you can visit www.lalithundalani.com

You can also click on the link below to join his VIP Facebook Group.

VIP Facebook group-VERSION 2.0 CLUB.

Or type https://www.facebook.com/groups/465486904543970/ in your web browser to join it.

Happy to Help You

Are you an **AMBITIOUS** person who wants to make it **BIG** and lead an **EXTRA-ORDINARY** life?

Are you feeling **STUCK** and looking for help?

If, yes then read on to know how I can help you unleash your true potential and become **UNSTOPPABLE**.

VERSION 2.0 is a holistic self-transformation program that works deep in your personality and helps you overcome the obstructions to become unstoppable.

It's a proven method, which gets you clarity on:

What should you do?

Why should you do?

How should you do?

Once you get the answers to the above questions, you transform into a better version of yourself.
Being consistently better every time will invariably make you the best.

Key Result Areas where this program works:

- Personal Growth
- Career
- Finance
- Health
- Relationship

The only commitment I would require from your end is **ACTION**.

Let's connect once you are ready to **ACT.**

To know more, book your FREE Session here>>Clarity Session
Or
visit **www.lalithundalani.com/Coaching t**o book it online.

See you soon.

Do you want to write a book and become the Best Selling Author?

According to a survey, 82% of people want to write a book, but only 5% can do so. To help you fulfill this dream, Lalit has created multiple programs & packages to help you in the journey of becoming a best-selling author.

If you are among the 82% majority and want to join the 5% minority, check the details of the below-mentioned programs & fulfill your dream.

Personal Author Mentorship Program

A personalized LIVE coaching program where you can learn to **WRITE & SELF-PUBLISH** your book in SIX simple steps.

For more details, visit: https://lalithundalani.com/author-personal-mentoring/

Self-Publishing Package

Have you written the book and need support in publishing it?

Then you can avail this package. Relax & focus on writing your next book or carry on other important stuff while we assist you in publishing your book.

For more details, visit: https://lalithundalani.com/self-publishing-services/

Indian Best-Seller Pack

Have your written and published your book and looking for a coveted Amazon#1 Best Seller tag for your book? We will get it for you.

For more details, visit: https://lalithundalani.com/indian-best-seller-package/

Global Best-Seller Pack

How about getting Amazon's #1 Best Seller tag in the US or UK? We can help you take your books to a global audience.

For more details, visit: https://lalithundalani.com/global-best-seller/

To know more details, you can contact us on https://lalithundalani.com/contact/ or write a mail to connect@lalithundalani.com. We will respond within 24 hours.

Preview of another book in Self-Transformation Series

"Hacking the Productivity"

Introduction

2 Scenarios

Scenario 1

Viru S B is a senior professor in one of the leading engineering colleges in India. He has been a topper all through his student life and a teacher par excellence. He is devoted to his work and utilizes every minute of the day to accomplish his tasks. The workaholism has helped him grow rather quickly, and as a result, he became the dean of his college earlier than the other senior colleagues. He is a guy obsessed with being productive and resorts to multitasking activities of another level. His quest to become most productive has given birth to some of the exceptional or rather weird habits. His eccentricities include wearing a shirt with velcro to save time on putting up the buttons, getting shaven while taking an afternoon nap, writing with both hands, and so on.

He is very punctual and disciplined to the core. He is a very average person with nothing odd in his lifestyle.

Scenario 2

RDC is a student in the same college who loves to celebrate life. He is a free-spirited person who wants to explore new things and hates sticking to a regimented schedule. He is not a workaholic and loves to have fun. He is not a multitasker and instead believes in doing one thing at a time with complete focus. He is a brilliant student, and despite devoting less time to studies, he is a college topper. In his first year at college, observing his carefree demeanor, no one expected him to be at the top of the tally. The results were quite shocking for everyone, including his friends, who were among the laggards despite working harder.

By now, most of you would have recognized that the above two scenarios are from a famous Bollywood movie of all times-3 IDIOTS. Viru S B was the character played by actor Boman Irani, and RDC is Ranchod das chanchad, the character played by actor Aamir khan. This movie is a perfect example of storytelling using the method of weaving in powerful messages. It has plenty of them.

Now coming back to our topic, why are we quoting the movie and the above scenarios? What is the relevance? Well, the above illustrations' objective is simple. The characters stated above are in direct contrast to each other and yet successful in their ways, as they can accomplish whatever they want. According to viru, his methods are correct, and one must utilize time efficiently to become more productive; hence, he hates people like RDC who don't have a regimented schedule. To RDC and others, Viru is suffering from OCD(Obsessive Compulsive Disorder) and FOMO(Fear of Mission Out), and therefore, he wants to be everywhere and do multiple things simultaneously.

So who is right and who is wrong? Well, if we ignore the eccentric habits of Viru for a while, both are right in their way. Both of them have habits and a schedule that works best for them and enhances their productivity. The purpose of quoting this example is to show that people are different, so are their working patterns, and ways to improve productivity and peak their performance. The observation is neither new nor a discovery. We all have known people in our student and work-life, how some of the students would excel in studies, sports, and other activities. In contrast, some others would have their focus areas identified clearly, which could either be academics, sports, music, play, etc.

The bottom line is that everyone is looking for ways to be successful; success can be achieved once you reach your performance's pinnacle and attain peak performance; being productive is a must. The ultimate goal or destination remains the same, but the path can be different. In our objective to become effective, we sometimes fall into the trap of emulating habits of successful people, which may or may not work for us. There is nothing wrong with following successful people, but the fact remains that it is not necessary that everyone can be productive by copying the habits of Steve Jobs or Bill Gates. If Bill gates achieved success by dropping out of college, thousands were in a similar situation but ended up nowhere; we don't know about them since they are not famous. Similarly, waking up early in the morning and be most productive might not work for everyone.

What this book holds for you?

This book is an attempt to present an alternate view to achieving peak performance by breaking common myths. As a result, you can understand yourself, identify the ways to boost productivity, and at the end of it, find what works best for you and, more importantly, what you can stick to without drastically altering your lifestyle.

Since we understand that an individual can't increase his/her productivity in isolation if the environment is not supportive, we have dedicated separate chapters to illustrate the productivity hacks and techniques for employees/professionals, businesses/organizations & students.

Whether you are a working professional, an employee, a self-employed professional, a business owner, or a student, this book holds something for you, and you will find it relevant. However, read this book only if you want to achieve peak performance in your life and currently feeling stuck.

--End of Preview—

Get your copy of the complete book >>>

Hacking The Productivity
On
www.Aamazon.com

Claim Your Free Gift!

As a token of appreciation for taking out time to read my book, I would like to offer you my E-BOOK VERSION 2.0 as a **FREE GIFT**

To claim your copy, pls visit
www.lalithundalani.com/coaching
Or
Mail to connect@lalithundalani.com

References

https://purposefocuscommitment.com/perseverance-story-be-mindful-of-distractions/
https://learningworksforkids.com/
https://www.successconsciousness.com/
https://www.guidedmind.com/blog/6-benefits-of-being-more-focused
https://learningtoolsforlife.com/the-importance-of-focus/
https://blog.trello.com/why-you-cant-focus-on-anything-plus-how-to-fix-it
https://vancruzer.com/stay-focused-at-work/
https://hbr.org/2017/05/your-brain-can-only-take-so-much-focus
https://susantaylor.org/blogs/neuroscience-of-focus/
https://www.focusatwill.com/app/pages/science-of-focus-concentrationbetter
https://www.physiopedia.com/Physical_Activity_and_Mental_Health
https://psychologycompass.com/
https://askinglot.com/what-are-the-7-nutrients
https://www.uwb.edu/business/faculty/sophie-leroy/attention-residue
http://www.bhagavatam-katha.com/mahabrarata-story-i-see-only-the-round-black-eye-of-the-bird/
https://purposefocuscommitment.com/mindset-story-kings-lesson-about-setting-priorities/
https://www.newstatesman.com/science-tech/coronavirus/2020/05/how-focus-concentration-pandemic-brain-motivation-apps-pomodoro
https://www.cognitivefxusa.com/blog/3-ways-stress-impacts-the-brain
https://psychologycompass.com/premium/focus/
https://dualdiagnosis.org/impulsive-bpd-alcoholism/
https://www.medicalnewstoday.com/articles/317815
https://thriveglobal.com/stories/the-power-of-connectedness-and-the-psychological-effects-of-social-distancing/
https://www.healthline.com/health/multiple-sclerosis/early-signs
https://www.healthline.com/health/concussion
https://www.healthline.com/health/dementia
https://www.nebraskaneurology.com/what-is-epilepsy/

https://www.healthline.com/health/insomnia
https://www.healthline.com/health/mental-health/depression-and-anxiety
https://www.insightfultherapytn.com/challenges/depression-and-anxiety
https://jamesclear.com/how-to-focus
https://www.entrepreneur.com/article/331424
https://positivepsychology.com/what-is-mindfulness/
https://www.mayoclinic.org/tests-procedures/meditation/in-depth/meditation/art-20045858
https://www.merriam-webster.com/dictionary/state
https://www.verywellmind.com/practice-focused-meditation-3144785
https://www.verywellmind.com/mindfulness-meditation-88369
https://www.sleepfoundation.org/how-sleep-works/what-happens-when-you-sleep
https://amerisleep.com/blog/sleep-impacts-brain-health/
https://www.helpguide.org/articles/healthy-living/the-mental-health-benefits-of-exercise.htm
https://optimistminds.com/benefits-of-exercise-on-mental-health/
https://www.helpguide.org/articles/healthy-living/the-mental-health-benefits-of-exercise.htm
https://www.lifehack.org/802571/distractions-at-work
https://www.huffpost.com/entry/focus-is-the-gateway-to-b_b_4206552
https://vllightingsolutions.com/how-lighting-solutions-affect-employees/
https://hbr.org/2018/08/4-strategies-for-overcoming-distraction
https://www.nytimes.com/2018/08/25/opinion/sunday/distracted-work-focus-productivity.html
https://time.com/5379422/why-being-lazy-is-actually-good-for-you/
https://www.fastcompany.com/90237319/how-to-solve-complex-problems-by-not-focusing-on-them
https://purposefocuscommitment.com/mindset-story-kings-lesson-about-setting-priorities/
https://www.forbes.com/sites/bryanrobinson/2021/02/12/how-to-focus-your-wandering-mind-and-amp-career-success/
https://neurosciencenews.com/enahnced-focus-neuroscience-6007/